The Wire

TV Milestones

CONTENTS

ACKNOWLEDGMENTS

I would like to thank Barry Grant and Jeannette Sloniowski for giving me the opportunity to contribute to this series and for their generous and helpful editorial assistance while working on drafts of the manuscript. Comments received from the press's anonymous readers were also helpful in clarifying my arguments. I am grateful for the work of Wayne State University Press's editors Annie Martin and Kristina Stonehill in shepherding this work from proposal through to book. I would also like to acknowledge Brock University's Chancellor's Chair for Research Excellence Fellowship, which contributed funds that assisted me in working on this project. Finally, thanks to Lisa Laframboise for editorial and indexing work and to Rob Macmorine for image capture.

"It's America, Man"

It's all in the game.
Omar Little, "All Prologue"

1

Although HBO's *The Wire* (2002–8) never achieved spectacular ratings or won an Emmy, journalists and critics frequently describe it as the best show that has appeared on television. It won a number of awards, the most prestigious of which was a 2004 Peabody Award. Walter Benn Michaels, praising the series in comparison to recent literary fiction that seems unable to grasp market logic's contemporary dominance, calls *The Wire* "the most serious and ambitious fictional narrative of the twenty-first century so far." Co-created by David Simon and Ed Burns, the series explores the far-reaching consequences of illegal drugs on the city of Baltimore and is influenced by Simon's *Homicide: A Year on the Killing Streets* (1991) and Simon and Burns's *The Corner: A Year in the Life of an Inner-City Neighborhood* (1997), both fact-based narratives written after extensive fieldwork in Baltimore. The series' reputation has only grown since the last of its five seasons aired, gaining new DVD audiences; President Obama even declared it his favorite show (Cook). Nominally a police drama, *The Wire* is distinguished by the complexity of its narrative and its refusal to restrict its focus to individual crimes isolated from the social context in which criminality is produced.

The Wire pushes television in new directions, taking advantage of the era of multiple, niche-targeted channels and HBO's freedom from both advertisers' priorities and FCC regulation. In a letter Simon wrote to HBO seeking support for the series (reproduced in *The Wire: Truth Be Told*), he argues that the show will do "something subversive" (Alvarez 33) with the reality of the cop-show universe, thus justifying its place on a network that was, at the time, defining itself by its ability to explore topics and situations a public network could not. Writing is at the show's center more than is typical for television: unlike network shows, *The Wire* was able to work with only fourteen writers over its sixty episodes, a consistency rarely achieved in television production. As well, three novelists known for their representations of inner-city life, Richard Price, Dennis Lehane, and George Pelecanos, were prominent contributors. Yet *The Wire*'s debts to television are as significant as those to fiction, and the show similarly worked with only twenty-six directors, seven of whom directed three or more episodes. Along with these conditions of production, Simon's own creative role should not be underemphasized: although he is credited with writing only 35 percent of the screenplays, he is acknowledged in the "story by" credit for 85 percent of the episodes, placing him in that emerging category of television "creator" able to retain an individual vision across the diffuse production mechanisms of television.

The Wire follows a group of police officers in Baltimore who investigate the city's drug trade. The first season is the most conventionally like a police drama, focusing on the Barksdale drug enterprise, but even here the complex characterization of criminals as well as police sets the show apart. *The Wire* plays with the serial format of television, a technique that achieved limited success on broadcast network shows such as *Murder One* (ABC 1995), which followed a single case over an entire

First murder in the series.

season, and *Boomtown* (NBC 2002), which depicted its cases from a variety of viewpoints (but did not fully characterizes its criminals, as does *The Wire*). Like other HBO series, including the flagship *The Sopranos* (1999–2007), *The Wire* builds its stories cumulatively, each individual episode contributing to larger stories about these characters and this world rather than necessarily containing within itself a climax and resolution. *The Wire* pushes this convention even further, allowing its first season case to conclude—in the sense that arrests are made and the investigation closed—but refusing to provide the sense of closure typical of police dramas. As the series main detectives, Lester Freamon (Clarke Peters) and Jimmy McNulty (Dominic West), go to arrest the main drug dealer, Avon Barksdale (Wood Harris), McNulty remarks, "This isn't as much fun as I thought it would be," and the season ends not with these arrests but with a vision of business-as-usual continuing. In later seasons,

The Wire shifts ever further away from the typical police drama formula, decentering the investigation to focus on other, contextual issues that produce the drug trade: the loss of work and economic stability (season two), institutional inertia and electoral politics (season three), an absence of social programs and a failed education system (season four), and, finally, an apathetic press that creates a misinformed public (season five).

The Wire structures each of its seasons to show the parallel pressures and failings of institutions structured around merciless market logic. This technique is used to make three points: first, it reveals the degree to which neoliberalism has collapsed all aspects of social life into the model of the marketplace; second, it reinforces an overarching theme, namely the refusal to demonize criminals and represent them as "other" to the rest of society; third, it provides a social critique of neoliberalist logic by showing the damage it does in a holistic way, insisting upon the connections among actions at different class levels that are generally obscured in mainstream economic discourse.

Jason Mittell's work in television genre theory is helpful for understanding *The Wire*'s relationship to the police drama form. Mittell argues that television genre is shaped by the intersections of multiple actors and sites of engagement: textual aesthetics and their relationship to previously established genres; the discourses of critics, academics, creators, and fans; production practices; regulatory policies; methods of distribution; and more. *The Wire* emerged in an era characterized by choice (multiple subscription channels, catering to specific niche markets) and branding (channels building an audience base through association with a larger lifestyle). As well, the DVD market and other platforms of distribution (such as Netflix) mean that television is now often conceived with the expectation of multiple and concentrated viewing, allowing much greater narrative complexity. Thus an audience can be built over time and the success of secondary distribution is as economically important as initial ratings. This context not only gave the series greater latitude to show violence and experiment with narrative pace than was typical of conditions of production and distribution but also gave Simon and Burns greater visibility vis-à-vis the show. Indeed, they, particularly Simon given his larger media role, can be classified with an emergent group of television professionals such as J. J. Abrams, Alan Ball, David Chase, and Joss Whedon who have become a "brand" themselves, known for specific thematic and aesthetic visions that produce a loyal audience, often across multiple distribution sites (film, cable, broadcast). Although television remains a collaborative medium, such individuals occupy a position we might call, following Foucault, the author function: they are not solely responsible for the text but serve as a site that unites various discourses into a coherent meaning. Simon is important for understanding *The Wire* not only because he occupies this place of the "author brand" but also because he has been active in publishing and lecturing about Baltimore, crime, capitalism, and growing economic inequalities in America, all of which are central to themes in *The Wire*.

5

If we follow Mittell in seeing this larger context of critical, fan, and industry statements as part of what shapes a show's genre, then Simon, in promoting *The Wire* and guiding viewer and critical responses to it, is an important element in this process I argue Simon offers a compelling reading of the show but is not the single locus of its meanings. The show is distinct from other police dramas in its focus on the systemic problems of racism and poverty in America that have created the drug culture and in its indictment of the limitations of existing institutions to redress these problems, as Simon argues. For example, *The Wire* is credited with inspiring other multilayered crime narratives such as the Danish series *Forbrydelsen* (DR 2007–) and the American remake *The Killing* (AMC 2011–); both, particularly the Danish series, are complex depictions of a single crime that trace their story over the entire season. Like *The Wire*, they show the influence of politics (in this case, a mayoral election) on investigative practice, and they also allude to larger social issues of racism and immigration (the original suspects are a Muslim in the Danish series and a Somali in the American one). Both are narratively complex, well-acted, and compelling dramas filmed with high production values. Neither, however, makes political and social issues the central theme. Instead, both can be understood as—albeit very good examples of—the police narrative that focuses on the lone crusading cop who remains dedicated to justice despite all obstacles, and both locate their affective energy with the grieving family. In contrast, *The Wire* is not a thriller about *a* crime but a quasi-journalistic analysis of crime as a social phenomenon.

At the same time, however, *The Wire* also exceeds Simon's conceptualization: it is more deeply indebted to television that preceded it than he admits, and it struggles to reconcile its commitment to offering a true picture of inner-city Baltimore with its investment in the narrative conventions of melodrama and tragedy. Simon frequently refers to the series as a "novel for television" and draws comparisons with literary works or writers (*Moby Dick,* Dickens, Balzac, Greek tragedy).[1] The tradition of American naturalism, with its emphasis on the inescapable forces of fate and the deterministic effects of environment, is perhaps the most apt, although seldom mentioned, analogue. The combination of this literary model with *The Wire's* commitment to showing systemic problems with American politics and capitalism often results in a diegesis that is without hope, potentially producing a sense of numbness (see Hsu) in its audience rather than activating a sense of engagement (Simon's stated intention).[2] By striving so strongly to reverse the emphasis on individualism that was the horizon for earlier police dramas and the popular conception of criminality they reinforced, *The Wire* risks evacuating agency from the lives of its mainly impoverished, African American characters, thereby instituting a new and differently damaging mythos of lives beyond salvation.

Simon argues that *The Wire* has distinct themes for each season, which he articulates in his introduction to *The Wire: Truth Be Told,* the series' official companion. Season one demonstrates that the "American war on drugs has mutated into a brutal suppression of the underclass" (11); season two extends this exploration of disenfranchisement to consider "the death of work and the betrayal of the working class" (11). The greater prominence of characters from city hall in season three provides "rumination on our political culture and the thin possibility of reform" (12), while season four looks at "the state of public education and, by extension, the American ideal of equality of opportunity" (12). Finally, season five presents "what remains of our media culture, a critique that makes plain why no one is left to do the hard work of explaining the precise nature of our national problems" (12). Atypical of series television, *The Wire* introduces new characters each season and is willing to kill some of its major characters from previous seasons, thus privileging the narrative—and its explicitly mapped-out themes— over the star appeal of individual actors. As a number of critics have noted, *The Wire* is ultimately less a police drama about law and order and more a comment on the consequences of capitalism. Simon wants the series to mobilize all the emotional power of fiction while at the same time presenting a "truth" of American life belied by much of the media. "It's fiction, I'm clear about that," he states in interview. "But at its heart it's journalistic" (Burkeman). Yet journalism and fiction make different demands on their material and their readers. This book argues that balancing the two is *The Wire's* most distinctive contribution and its Achilles' heel.

Situating *The Wire*

I think you need a lot of context to seri- **9**
ously examine anything.
Gus Haynes, "Unconfirmed Reports"

*T*he Wire's critical acclaim is based on its social realism. For example, Jacob Weisberg proclaims,

> No other program has ever done anything remotely like what this one does, namely to portray the social, political, and economic life of an American city with the scope, observational precision, and moral vision of great literature. . . . The drama repeatedly cuts from the top of Baltimore's social structure to its bottom, from political fund-raisers in the white suburbs to the subterranean squat of a homeless junkie. . . . *The Wire's* political science is as brilliant as its sociology. It leaves *The West Wing,* and everything else television has tried to do on this subject, in the dust.

What is obscured by such hyperbolic praise, however, is the degree to which *The Wire* achieves such success through its sophisticated engagement with television as a medium as much as through elements drawn from literature. Building on Raymond Williams's idea that we experience television as flow, a fluid movement across segments of programs, advertising, news, and the like, John Ellis argues that television is best understood as a mode of working-through in the psychoanalytic sense. Television, he argues, "can be seen as a vast mechanism for processing the raw data of news reality into more narrativized, explained forms" (55).

One of the things that distinguishes television from film, Ellis contends, is the more open-ended structure of television narratives, a characteristic most evident in the never-ending plotlines of genres such as soap operas but present also in the resolved narratives of episodic police dramas in the sense that each week one returns to view the same detectives solving the next crime. This openness is for Ellis "television's distinctive contribution to the modern age—a relatively safe area in which uncertainty can be entertained (and can be entertaining)" (64).[1] Such analyses lend weight to the idea that a television series could fill the gap in contemporary culture left empty by the failure of news media. Television is already a medium that blurs the line between fiction and reality, and the packaging of difficult themes as entertainment may enable some viewers to confront them. Drawing on Justin Lewis's study of television audiences, *The Ideological Octopus,* David Morley argues that "the world of television fiction in general is much closer to most people's lives than that presented in the news" (141), in large part because they feel the characters in, for example, soap operas face personal dilemmas and moral issues that readers connect with their own lives. Conversely, "the world of television news is much more remote in all senses; it is a socially distant world populated by another race of special or 'elite' persons, the world of 'them' not 'us'" (141). Thus, rather than seeing *The Wire*'s transformation of pressing social issues into fictional form as a trivialization, I suggest that we see its revising of the police drama as a way to make the largely middle-class viewers of HBO[2] feel connected to the world of economically disadvantaged inner-city residents, what Simon calls "the America left behind . . . that portion of our country that we have discarded" (Alvarez 9).[3]

Police Television

The series' dependence upon—as much as divergence from—the established tradition of police drama is significant for understanding this ideological work. Police dramas are simultaneously reflections of and contributions toward shaping contemporary attitudes about criminality and state power, as Stuart Hall et al. established in their groundbreaking volume *Policing the Crisis* (1978). The critical, at times cynical vision of the police department dramatized by *The Wire* would not have been possible without the crime drama that came before. As Sophie Fugle notes, *The Wire*'s "refusal to grant closure, or even to suggest what form such closure might take" not only distinguishes it from earlier police dramas but at times constitutes a direct attack upon their simplistic visions of the causes of—and solutions to—criminality.

At the same time, however, the series owes a significant debt to earlier dramas.[4] For example, *Naked City* (ABC 1958–63) depicted crime as emerging from social rather than moral problems, although it nonetheless retained a perspective that privileged the individual rather than the system as the locus of causality. Similarly, in its focus on the minutiae of police work and especially the careful recording and processing of data, *The Wire* owes a debt to early procedural shows such as *Dragnet* (NBC 1951–59). Like *The Wire*, *Dragnet* is characterized by a close relationship to contemporary police practice and an obsessive attentiveness to procedural details. Yet while *Dragnet* was shaped by Jack Webb's conservative vision and depicted "crime [as] a force lacking explicable motivations, clear patterns, or even reason, but posing an omnipresent danger from which the

11

police must constantly defend society" (Mittell 138), *The Wire* insists upon all the contingent, contextual, and social explanations of crime excised by the earlier series. Although *The Wire* works against the grain of American television drama, its use of conventions of realism on television for social critique is not unprecedented. In 1960s British television, as Robin Nelson argues, "experiments of Loach and Garnett, taking lightweight 16 mm cameras out of the studio into actual environments and improvising with non-actors, increased a sense of television's capacity 'to show things as they really are'" (170). *The Wire* similarly uses Baltimore locals and films on locations that *are* rather than *mimic* the neighborhoods in which its stories are set. Many of its visual aesthetics mirror those of Hollywood cinema, but it nonetheless strives for documentary realism in its narratives.

The series seems at times to be a counterargument to the dominant perspective embodied in the other heirs to early forensic procedurals, series such as *CSI* (CBS 2000–) and its franchise of spin-offs. *The Wire* rejects their only loosely connected episodes, which situate viewers with the investigative team, rather than within a larger context in which crime is part of a social structure, and their fetishization of evidence as the source of Truth, which works against any systemic analysis of criminality. Michele Byers and Val Marie Johnson link forensic investigation narratives to neoliberalism and "governing through crime" owing to such narratives' work in "legitimating policing powers as essential and moral-scientific" (xvii). Such series refuse "the social as a realm informing human action, conflict, and solutions except through the local workings of forensic teams" (xvii–xviii) and focus on "individual responsibility of crime fighter and criminal" (xviii). Nicholas Dobson suggests that the *CSI* franchise is a descendant of series such as *Miami Vice* (NBC 1984–90), which privilege a slick style characterized by bright colors, frequent chase scenes, energetic nondiegetic sound, and attractive actors rather than narrative or theme.

CSI's fetishization of forensic evidence, its montage sequences of attractive lab technicians performing tests accompanied by nondiegetic music, and its frequent use of digital effects to visualize the crime in extreme close-up—the "camera" even penetrating the body to show tissue or bone damage—continues this MTV-like tradition of police dramas and contrasts significantly with *The Wire*'s visual aesthetic as well as with its themes. Other than in final montage sequences that end each season, *The Wire* uses only diegetic music and typically focuses on faces of individuals in conversation, favoring shot and countershot sequences for most significant dialogue. In contrast to *CSI,* the bodies on *The Wire* are rarely shown in close-up, and when they are, such shots are often of faces, the camera pausing to allow us to contemplate the death of often-known individuals rather than providing a voyeuristic view of injuries. *The Wire*'s visual representations of police work emphasize paper trails, not chase scenes or gunfire, often accompanied by voice-overs that explain the procedures. The most prominent visual trademark within the series is the slow zoom: either in to a character's face to show reaction or out from a scene to establish its relationship to the larger context of the city.

Kevin Bonnycastle argues that *CSI* is "dependent upon eclipsing the needy and disappearing all dispossessed groups that expose the contradictions at the heart of new governing rationalities" (160–61), noting that this ideological function works in direct contrast to *The Wire,* whose mission is to make visible the damage of neoliberal economics. The frequent satiric references to forensic work within the series suggest that its writers, too, are aware that they are working in an opposing paradigm: few scenes involve the analysis of trace evidence, and it is made clear that, absent knowing the *social* structure of the drug enterprise, such forensic evidence could not be meaningfully interpreted. Further, police in *The Wire* must confront the economic realities of how investigations—and lab work—are

13

funded, including the political hierarchy between crimes made priorities and those involving victims "dead in a zip code that does not fucking matter" (Landsman in "Dead Soldiers"). The trace evidence for twenty-two murder victims found in vacant houses at the end of season four, for example, is mixed up by an inexperienced, temporary lab tech ("The Dickensian Aspect"), making it impossible to ascertain from which scene any was taken, but this problem goes unnoticed because the "Lab can't keep up with this year's scenes" (Landsman in "Not for Attribution"). Indeed, even when DNA evidence finally does permit police to identify the murderer of another victim, the investigating detective is able to make the DNA match only because he knows the social context (having requested child social services records on one of the people involved) and because his lab tests are funded by surreptitiously using the case number for another, priority investigation.

The series *Criminal Minds* (CBS 2005–) also seems targeted by this final story line, the basis for season five: the priority case involves a serial killer targeting homeless men. This killer, however, does not exist but is manufactured by McNulty and Freamon in order to gain resources to continue their investigation of drug dealer Marlo Stanfield (Jamie Hector). Frustrated by city cutbacks that required them to shut down their investigation, these detectives produce a media sensation through their fiction of a sexually motivated serial killer, the press coverage of which ensures that they are adequately funded. Marlo really is a serial killer, they rationalize, but one whose targets— predominantly black men in the drug trade in Baltimore—are not of sufficient interest to politicians and the public. The priorities of crime dramas such as *Criminal Minds* and the vision of law and order they market to the public are thus satirized by this story line, and the fictional Baltimore public is indicted as sharing the worldview that makes cases like those profiled in *Criminal Minds* of greater interest.[5]

Far from the typical story of justice prevailing over criminality, *The Wire* is instead an exploration of the ways in which market and election-cycle logics have invaded all aspects of social life. The series' ensemble cast and avoidance of a clear protagonist further emphasize its interest in systemic rather than individual analysis of the drug war (inevitably, however, as demonstrated by online fan postings, viewers connect with individual characters, which perhaps suggests a limitation for television fiction as a mode of social critique). In contrast to neoliberal decontextualization, then, *The Wire* encapsulates an argument that Simon and Burns make at length in *The Corner*: the war on drugs requires more than prisons; it requires the recognition "that pure, unbridled capitalism be regarded not as the equivalent of social policy, but as a powerful economic system in need of humane constraint" (376). Its reliance on an ensemble cast connects *The Wire* with earlier police dramas such as *Hill Street Blues* (NBC 1981–87) and *NYPD Blue* (ABC 1993–2005). The former is particularly significant for opening up the representation of police to show officers as complex characters with flaws rather than as the paragons of moral virtue typical of earlier series. Further, *Hill Street Blues* marks a shift in television police drama through "its honest assessment of urban policing and inner-city life during the 1980s" (Vest 24), although it continues to follow in a tradition that bifurcates the world into an "us" of police and law-abiding citizens and a "them" of an often-demonized criminal class. The ensemble camaraderie of this series was in part achieved by presenting a police force allied against the "inhuman conditions" of the city, which is called a "war zone" in the pilot episode (Vest 29).

The Wire is careful to add as much complexity to its criminal characters as it provides for the police, stressing the parallels between individuals trying to accommodate themselves to the institutions they must serve rather than highlighting their differences as people on opposite sides of the law. Individual characters from both contingents are shown to have families, individual moral codes, and capacities for pettiness and for generosity. A seemingly facetious acknowledgment of the more bifurcated world view of *Hill Street Blues* is incorporated into the roll call scenes from season three: Lieutenant Dennis Mello, played by former Baltimore homicide sergeant Jay Landsman, updates the iconic "let's be careful out there" to "don't get captured."

The Wire's debt to *NYPD Blue* is predominantly the space that series created for talking about race in police dramas. Largely the story of the redemption of Officer Andy Sipowicz (Dennis Franz) from his initial characterization as an alcoholic racist, the series articulated anxieties of a white male culture whose hegemony was waning. *NYPD Blue* cast nonwhite actors in roles beyond criminals and similar stereotypes characteristic of their appearance on earlier police series. Nonetheless, it remained focused predominantly on the narrative of the white protagonists, and indeed actor James McDaniel, who played Sipowicz's African American boss, referred to himself as "the highest paid extra on television" (qtd. in Gibb and Sabin). Similarly, as Vest points out, the show fails to interrogate institutional, social, economic, and political causes of racism, poverty, and injustice in favor of its examination of individual characters and their capacity for change. *The Wire* responds to and revises this vision in a numbers of ways. First, it has a racially diverse cast that features significant roles for African American as well as white actors. Second, both police and criminal characters are given significant scenes that show them as full human beings rather than as caricatures. Finally, although the show is initially anchored around the white Jimmy McNulty—a concession to HBO marketing about which both Simon and West have expressed uneasiness in DVD commentary and interview—*The Wire* works to undermine this centrality in the first season, and in subsequent seasons this role is increasingly less central.

The Wire "disavows the idea that a few heroic individuals

could solve the entrenched problems of a city like Baltimore" (McMillan 62), which not only differentiates it from other police procedurals that focus on the crusading cop but also prevents the McNulty figure from dominating the nonwhite characters. Indeed, although McNulty likes to narrate himself as both the most intelligent and the most committed officer on the unit, his hubris is as frequently undermined, and the entire series builds toward his epiphany in season five that he was never as crucial as he believed himself to be. In the first episode, the investigative detail is formed through McNulty's machinations, which prompt a judge to question what lay behind the death of a witness. McNulty presents himself as motivated entirely by justice, condemning the apathy of other members of the department, but when another cop is later shot he guiltily admits that ego was his primary motivation, only to be told by his African American commander, Cedric Daniels (Lance Reddick), "Did you think we all didn't know?" ("Cleaning Up"). Similarly, throughout the first season the important breaks in the case come from the mostly silent and meticulous work of African American detective Freamon, who carefully follows up on a boxing lead to find the first photo of Avon, notes a number written on an abandoned stash house wall that establishes the first wiretap, and, most crucially, knows that the key to arresting those responsible comes from following the money away from the street corners rather than following the drugs into the projects.

The most obvious precursor for *The Wire* is *Homicide: Life on the Street* (NBC 1993–99), a series based on Simon's eponymous journalistic narrative and upon which he worked as a writer. What distinguishes *The Wire* from this earlier series is its focus on crime as a product of systemic economic and other social forces and its relentless critique of these forces, something *Homicide* was less able to explore given its dependence on broadcast television economics and its consequent need to generate a large audience while courting advertisers. In his

Lack of resources—lack of systemic solutions

introduction to *The Wire: Truth Be Told,* Simon complains that during script production for *Homicide* the writers were asked to provide "victories" (12) and "life-affirming moments" (13) that he felt were at odds with the reality he observed in Baltimore. DVD commentaries on the *Homicide* series frequently refer to the writers' struggle to negotiate between the story they wanted to tell and NBC executives' vision of what would make a profitable series. The bleaker vision of *Homicide*'s first four seasons (in which a number of cases remain open) contrasts with the last three seasons, during which new characters were frequently introduced in an effort to broaden the series' appeal and cases were more definitively resolved.

Further, the network stressed plots that concluded in a single episode and wanted criminals to be arrested in most of the cases. In a panel discussion included on the season seven

DVDs, Barry Levinson, Tom Fontana, David Simon, and others reveal that NBC insisted that the extended story line of drug dealer Luther Mahoney (Erik Dellums) end with his death. In *The Wire,* a more realistic vision is possible: most of the investigations end inconclusively and almost all of the major drug dealers remain on the streets or are killed through circumstances unrelated to police activity. Tom Fontana's role as a writer for *Homicide* also points to another overlooked influence on *The Wire,* his earlier HBO series *Oz* (1997–2003). *The Wire* shares with *Oz* a concern with understanding criminals as full and complex human beings rather than as caricatures and with situating discourses on law and order within a context of economics.[6] Maria Siano, in her study of representations of crime in television dramas, credits *Oz* with marking a shift from series that predominantly represented criminals as outsiders toward series that show them as part-of rather than other-to society (4). In addition, *Oz*'s direct engagement with race and its multiracial cast, as well as its embedded commentary on the prison system's role in suppressing a racialized underclass, align it with the social vision of *The Wire.*

Although *The Wire* is thematically similar to *Oz,* it adopts a different visual mode. *Oz*'s most distinctive characteristic is its break with the conventions of narrative realism through the framing device of the monologues of Augustus Hill (Harold Perrineau), which contextualize the drama presented within the diegesis by referring to things such as historical events that marked shifts in attitudes toward criminality, statistics about the rates of incarceration in the contemporary United States, or other information about the prison system potentially not known to the series' audience (the use of criminal labor, disenfranchisement of convicted felons, and the like). Thus, *Oz* combines an intense drama, often sharing many of the conventions of melodrama or the soap opera in its focus on individual relationships, with a postmodern framing that prompts the reader to connect this narrative with the real social world.

The Wire never breaks its fictional frame and indeed is predominantly filmed in a style that belies the existence of the camera and strives for the high-quality visual mise-en-scène of Hollywood cinema. The shots are carefully composed, contributing as much to characterization and atmosphere as do dialogue and plot, and often offer moments of visual beauty amid the horrors of what they depict, such as the flashing blue lights of police cars reflected in the blood trail filmed in close-up in the series' opening shot, or the careful emergence of Omar (Michael K. Williams) from shadow into visibility, only to fade back into darkness again, his glowing cigarette tip the last visible element ("Bad Dreams"). As with the use of music, when we are prompted to notice the visual framing of the shot this is done from within the diegesis, such as by collapsing the screen image with the view seen by one of the monitoring technologies deployed by the police: a telephoto camera lens that briefly snaps and freezes the image; surveillance monitors that, on occasion, switch to black-and-white footage; and close-ups of computer screens whose graphics represent the rise and fall of voices from wiretapped conversations we hear.

Frequently information is conveyed only visually, and such is the series' commitment to a loyal and attentive viewership that in later seasons significant information is conveyed merely by glances between characters, information that can be decoded only by a viewer who recognizes each and knows their histories. At other times the care taken with the image enhances the viewing pleasure for attentive readers, such as Omar's T-shirt proclaiming "I Am the American Dream," seen in "Storm Warnings," his reading of *Ghettoheat,* an anthology of inner-city poetry, while imprisoned in "Unto Others," or the name of the pleasure-cruise boat, *Capital Gains,* towed by McNulty in "Ebb Tide." Perhaps the most amusing example of conveying narrative by visual exchange is the scene in "Old Cases" where McNulty and fellow detective Bunk Moreland (Wendell Pierce) solve a crime by visiting the crime scene, looking at visual evidence, and reenacting what happened, communicating with one another only through variations of the word "fuck."[7] Each season ends with a montage of scenes of Baltimore, involving characters and other shots of ongoing Baltimore life, that serve two important purposes: first, they undermine any sense of narrative closure, as without fail these montages reinforce for us the knowledge that despite whatever arrests have happened, the drug trade goes on; second, they insist that these stories take place in a real city, that the fictional Baltimore echoes and haunts the material city. Such visual strategies further speak to *The Wire's* status as a series made possible only by the context of premium, subscription viewing of television in a manner more closely allied with the detailed attention paid to film than with the sporadic and flickering attention, disrupted by advertising, that characterized television viewing in an earlier context of production. *The Wire* strives for the immersive viewing experience more often attributed to film through its attention to visual details and its refusal to disrupt the narrative experience with metatextual intrusions, a technique used, for example, in Simon and Burns's earlier series *The Corner* (2000), to achieve a pseudo-documentary effect.

Further, unlike its precursor *Homicide, The Wire* does not use the conventions of hand-held cameras, poorly framed images, and grainy footage to mimic documentary realism, a strategy adopted by the contemporary (and quite differently innovative) series *The Shield* (FX 2002–8). Instead, *The Wire* strives for a social realism like that of the nineteenth-century naturalist fiction to which it has been compared, using the devices of artifice to capture in rich detail a reality other than that experienced by most of its audience. The series is filmed mostly on location rather than in dedicated sets and frequently in outdoor locations filmed in wide-angle and long shots. Such techniques relentlessly remind us that the drug trade happens in a real city, insisting that these neighborhoods involve life beyond the drug trade and presenting rounded characters rather than crime drama stereotypes. For example, while minding their drug trade, teenagers Bodie (J. D. Williams) and Poot (Tray Chaney) discuss girlfriends, play chess, and speculate about the inventor of Chicken McNuggets—who, the more cynical D'Angelo (Lawrence Gilliard) informs them, is most likely still working "in the basement" ("The Detail"), the profit having gone to the corporation. Frequently the series uses long shots from a high perspective that pull back from some site of violence or crime and tilt up to show the downtown skyline, city hall, or an affluent neighborhood, juxtaposing the poor and abandoned neighborhoods with sites of gentrification and thus connecting the two. Similarly, the series frequently uses intercut scenes to establish parallels between institutions of various sorts, such as the cuts between Comstat police meetings and Barksdale drug crew meetings throughout season three, another mechanism for insisting on the connections among rather than gaps between these aspects of life in Baltimore.

"The Buys"

The season one episode "The Buys," written by David Simon and directed by Peter Medak, demonstrates *The Wire's* revision of police drama, its articulation of social and political themes, and its attentive use of detail in an early episode whose full significance is made evident only once the entire series has been viewed. The episode opens in the Pit, the central courtyard of project housing that is one site of Barksdale drug distribution, currently managed by Avon's nephew D'Angelo and a crew of adolescent boys, most significantly Bodie and Wallace (Michael B. Jordan). This scene builds on a binary characterization between D'Angelo and Bodie: D'Angelo is born into the drug enterprise and uncomfortable with the violence around him; Bodie is without family (we later learn he was raised by a grandmother, his mother dead from an overdose) and anxious to excel in the only social enterprise he knows. The day's drug shipment is late and an addict approaches first D'Angelo, then Bodie, asking for supply: Bodie reacts aggressively, berating the man for needing a high at nine in the morning, and yells, "Get the fuck out of here!" The camera swings to D'Angelo, who challenges Bodie's attitude. Bodie replies, "He's a goddamned drug addict," to which D'Angelo notes, "You're a goddamned drug dealer." In the ensuing discussion, D'Angelo tries to insist that there should remain something human in the exchange, that they can deal drugs without adopting a predatory attitude toward their customers. The camera remains on D'Angelo's face as he passionately argues for a different way, then swings quickly to Bodie, who just looks off into the distance, unconvinced. The conversation wanes as Bubbles (Andre Royo), a police informant, approaches. The scene cuts to a long and high shot of their group and then to the police on the roof watching, who are shown only briefly before the opening credits.

23

As this opening sequence shows, *The Wire* privileges the social context in which crime happens over investigative forensics or heroic grandstanding by police. Indeed, the next two scenes of the police department both emphasize its failings: first a discussion among senior officials of how to cover up an assault on a teenage boy by a drunken officer, Pryzbylewski (Jim True-Frost), and another in which McNulty cajoles two alcoholic and apathetic coworkers into searching housing files for a picture of Avon. This episode demonstrates the writers' skill in composing scenes that both forward the action of a particular episode and create space for social commentary. For example, drug addict Bubbles critiques the undercover attire of Detective Sydnor (Corey Parker Robinson) and thus draws attention to consequences of drug addiction—Sydnor is sufficiently dirty and ill clothed but would be thinner if truly addicted and would long since have pawned the wedding ring he still wears. The theft of a drug shipment by Omar, a Robin Hood figure who steals from drug dealers, provides the pretext for cutting and hence diluting the product as they wait for a "re-up," leading to a discussion between D'Angelo and Stringer Bell (Idris Elba) about the entrenched power of the drug trade. D'Angelo worries that their product is inferior, but Stringer notes, "Shit is weak, but shit is weak all over. Thing is, no matter what we call heroin, it going get sold." Stringer sits behind a desk, looking every inch the corporate CEO he wants to be, as he counts money and continues, "This shit right here, D, it's forever." This scene opens with an establishing shot of Stringer sitting at his desk in the background, with a pile of money dominating the foreground.

Three significant events happen in this episode critical for understanding the series, although their significance can be fully appreciated only upon rewatching, a quality typical of the kind of attention *The Wire* demands of its viewers. The most significant scene is a checkers game between Wallace and Bodie conducted as they wait for their late shipment. D'Angelo inter-

Stringer argues the heroin trade is forever.

venes and insists that chess is a much better game and—since they have a chessboard—they should learn it. Bodie is initially resistant but quickly develops an interest as D'Angelo begins to explain the chess pieces through analogy to "the game," as they all call the drug business. Wallace, in contrast, is immediately intrigued and open to knowing a world wider than the one his circumstances permit. A medium shot includes all three, Wallace on the left, the chessboard with D'Angelo behind it in the center, and Bodie to the right. This visual positioning mirrors D'Angelo's status as mediator between the perspectives embodied in Wallace and Bodie. Wallace remains open and most like the teenager he is, curious about the world and mirroring D'Angelo's own desire for another way. Bodie is resigned to the world as he finds it: he sits further from the table than Wallace, originally slouching back as compared to Wallace, who learns forward. Although Wallace is the one most interested in learning, Bodie is the more intelligent character. D'Angelo explains that the king is like Avon, the queen like his second-in-command, Stringer, and the knight like the stash house for drugs and cash, which they regularly move. Bodie realizes that he is a pawn but focuses on the minute chance that a pawn will be promoted to a more versatile and powerful piece, even though D'Angelo tells him that "the king stay the king." In quick succession Bodie tries a number of scenarios he feels might lead to winning the game: asking how one gets to be king and what is gained from a pawn crossing the entire board, first hoping it means he wins and then qualifying, "If I make it to the end, I'm top dog."

D'Angelo patiently corrects him, explaining, "It ain't like that. Pawns, man, in the game, they get capped quick. They be out early." Unconvinced, Bodie slouches back and looks from under his hood to insist, "Unless they some smart-ass pawns." In the rest of the episode, and throughout the series, we see evidence of Bodie acting in "the game" as he does when learning chess, demonstrating his intelligence and looking for ways

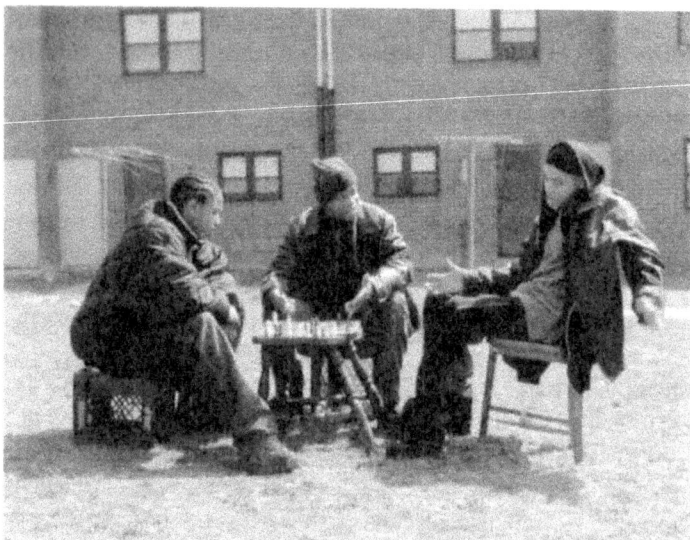

D'Angelo teaches Bodie and Wallace chess.

to rise in status. When Omar breaks into their stash house and robs them, only Bodie keeps his head and coolly looks around, noticing details about the robbery instead of looking at the ground in fear of being shot. D'Angelo is not even present, having gone out to buy food, and is later berated by Avon's enforcer, Wee-Bey (Hassan Johnson), in a scene whose visual composition echoes the framing of Wallace, D'Angelo, and Bodie before the chessboard. D'Angelo and Wee-Bey stand arguing while Bodie, sitting on a chair turned backward, leans forward and is framed between them. Wee-Bey blames D'Angelo for not preventing the robbery and, worse, not knowing any details that would enable retaliation. Unasked, Bodie contributes that he heard the name Omar and saw a white van. Like Freamon, who also emerges as a thoughtful analyst in this episode, Bodie is established here as precisely the "smart-ass pawn" he aspires to be. Such characterization—especially in the context of the entire series when we know of his death at approximately the age of twenty—refuses to allow us to dismiss the criminal characters as one-dimensional and conveys a sense of tragedy about their limited prospects. *The Wire* will return to this image in season four's "Final Grades," in which an older Bodie finally acknowledges, "This game is rigged. We be like the little bitches on the chessboard" shortly before he is killed. Both Wallace and D'Angelo will also be dead by that time, deaths depicted as inevitable: Bodie lives longer because his intelligence and harshness better equip him to negotiate their social world, but in the end death or imprisonment is the fate of those whose lives are confined to the drug trade, as we are repeatedly reminded over the course of the series.

Although such a reading obviously cannot be made upon first viewing, my point is that one of the things that distinguishes *The Wire* from other television is its willingness to de-

Bodie provides information on the drug heist.

vote screen time to matters whose full significance can emerge only episodes or seasons later. In this it is perhaps more like the miniseries than serial television, a division that is increasingly blurred with the rise of story-arc formats. Each episode develops several plotlines simultaneously, demonstrating the power of what Glen Creeber calls long-form drama, a mode he argues draws upon the narrative openness associated with the television soap opera, merged with other dramatic forms. *The Wire* is not the first or only series to make use of this format: *Twin Peaks* (ABC 1990–91), *Babylon 5* (PTEN 1994–98), and *24* (Fox 2001–10) all experimented with season and series story arcs. Yet *The Wire* tells the most intricate story to date and refuses to provide the sorts of cues (such as "previously on" introductory segments) designed to help viewers negotiate such series. Responding to critiques that the soap opera aesthetics of long-form narratives destroy "the political and critical potential of television drama," Creeber suggests that these qualities of openness and emotional investment make long-form drama "an unusually versatile vehicle for exploring and investigating the philosophical nature of history" (23). Similarly, attentiveness to characterization and narration of lives over an extended period of time, techniques evident in "The Buys," contribute to *The Wire*'s ability to comment in a meaningful way on the drug trade in Baltimore. Discussing typical police dramas, Ann Dunn argues that their repetitiveness, which allows a series to continue week after week with new iterations of crime, "*normalises* the central problematic of the program" and thus, in her example, *The Bill* (1984–2010), "racism, poverty and dysfunctional families are everyday phenomena, but crime is an intrusion, an upset" (138). *The Wire,* through its careful contextualization of the social world that produces the drug trade and the crime that goes with it, has a different effect: crime, too, is normalized in the sense that like poverty and racism, it is shown to be the result of systemic problems and thus to require systemic solutions.

Not only is the neat wrapping up of each case more typical of episodic police drama rejected by *The Wire,* but such an attitude toward policing is shown to perpetuate rather than discourage crime. "The Buys" concludes with a raid on the projects based on inadequate information obtained from hasty surveillance and done to provide "the circus," in Daniels's words, demanded by his superiors as a dramatic demonstration of the efficacy of drug enforcement. This scene, which most resembles typical police dramas, shows police cars speeding up to project housing, people running across the courtyard and being tackled by police, and doors being smashed in by battering rams. In the end, however, they have nothing to show for the raid. The stash has been moved, as Bodie quietly informs Wee-Bey, and were it not for the attentiveness of Freamon, who notes D'Angelo's pager number on the former stash house wall, nothing would have been gained. Thus, "The Buys" ends in defeat for the typical formulaic police drama episode but does so in a way that establishes the need to understand the economic and social dimensions of the drug trade.

29

The Parallel Economy

We used to make shit in this country,
build shit. Now we just put our hand in
the next guy's pocket.

Frank Sobotka, "Bad Dreams"

The conclusion to season one demonstrates that *The Wire* works against the grain of traditional police drama in its refusal to allow the closing of the case to suggest victory: although some members of the Barksdale organization go to jail, business continues. Season two marks a more radical departure as the action shifts from the projects to the docks and narrative focus from inner-city residents to working-class stevedores. Yet this change makes sense from the point of view of the series' argument about the drug culture: the rise of the drug trade is directly traceable to the collapse of economic alternatives for impoverished citizens, and the justice system's war on drugs is best understood as a war on this underclass.

Season two makes this argument in its story of the fall of the local International Brotherhood of Stevedores (IBS) union under the leadership of Frank Sobotka (Chris Bauer), who becomes involved in smuggling to raise cash in the vain hope of saving the working culture of the Baltimore docks. Frank's contact, Spiros Vondopoulos (Paul Ben-Victor), works with The Greek (Bill Raymond), who ultimately proves to be the major supplier of drugs to Baltimore, thus connecting this season's narrative with the interrogation of drug culture throughout *The Wire*. The season opens with the discovery of a body floating in the harbor, that of a murdered woman from Eastern Europe smuggled in to work in the sex trade. Her murder is eventually solved, but that is not what propels the narrative; instead, season two is the tragic tale of the fall of the union, making evident one of the central themes of the series: the drug culture is an economy that parallels the legitimate one, the only economy left for an impoverished class of citizens no longer relevant to financial capital. At times the parallels and disjunctions between these two economies are represented to humorous effect. For example, in "Boys of Summer" Marlo's enforcer Snoop (Felicia Pearson) enters a hardware store to purchase a nail gun, a tool they are using to board up vacant homes in which they are hiding bodies. She engages in a long discussion with the clerk about the relative merits of each model, exchanging comments about the number of contracting jobs she works each month and the like. Finally she settles on a gunpowder-activated rather than battery-charged tool, and it is only when she pays with $800 cash and talks about recognizing the power of a 22-caliber bullet to break bones that the clerk is jarred from his assumptions.

There is more that connects the Polish American stevedore community with the hegemony of the drug culture in African American neighborhoods than merely their common association with Spiros, however, and this "more" is precisely the socioeconomic context of the drug trade that *The Wire* takes pains to map. In season one, the police investigation was closed due to political pressure, which emerged when the investigation traced connections between Avon's drug money and two sites of supposedly legitimate finance: campaign contributions and real-estate development. One of the central struggles in season two concerns Frank's efforts to lobby legislators to dredge the canal and refurnish the grain pier, thereby allowing more ships and more work to come to the Baltimore docks. His major antagonist is developer Andy Krawczyk (Michael Willis), who plans to build a condominium called The Granary on this spot. Frank's turn to smuggling is explained by his desire to protect his union: when asked to go without payment for a time to wait out the police investigation, he angrily insists, "I got things happening with my union. Right now. Not a fucking month from now when the legislative session is over. Now" ("Duck and Cover"). We never see Frank spend money on himself but instead see it go to bribes, the lobbyist, and an informal social safety net for down-on-their-luck stevedores as "change" for their bar tab. Frank comes into conflict with African American stevedore Nat Coxson (Luray Cooper), who believes that

33

Loss of labor in the empty docks.

dredging the canal is beyond their grasp and prioritizes the grain pier; Nat rejects a vision of money as the only viable form of speech and promotes change achieved by writing to their legislators. Although Frank's choice to become involved with smuggling is shown to have tragic consequences, Nat's view is far more naive, as the connection via Krawczyk to the themes of season one suggests.

Back in the Day

Frank is blind to the changing world and the problems of a younger generation without seniority for whom even the remaining scraps of manual labor will never be enough to build a life. This story of trapped youth is told primarily through the mirrored narratives of Frank's son, Ziggy (James Ransone), and his nephew, Nick (Pablo Schreiber). Both are in their twenties but still live with their parents since they have no economic prospects: Nick lives in the basement and this cramped set, where he frequently bumps his head on the ceiling, makes literal his situation. Both become involved with the drug trade: Ziggy is continually emasculated and eventually goes to jail for murder when, in frustration and rage at his impotence, he shoots the last person who humiliated him. Nick more successfully negotiates his move into the drug culture, but it is repeatedly made clear that it is only his connection with Vondas, a known player, that protects him from its violence. Nick is aggressively resentful of the fact that his only economic prospect is selling drugs. As he walks along the docks complaining about the lack of work for someone at his level of seniority, he insists that he does not want to be "like some project nigger" ("Hot Shots"). Later, when he negotiates to distribute his supply, he refuses to mimic the African American styles of speech adopted by the white boys on the street, looks ashamed when a woman glares at them from her window, and ends the exchange by pronouncing that, despite their comportment, these men are white, as is

Ziggy lashes out against lack of opportunity, disappears into the prison system.

he. Nick goes on to qualify that he is, unlike them, "not hanging on the corner don't give a shit white" ("Backwash") but rather IBS, a proud tradition of white, working-class culture.

Other scenes reinforce that for Nick and his generation the viability of Polish working-class life remains tantalizingly visible if just out of reach: Nick and his girlfriend look to buy a house and find that his aunt's house, sold by the family when she died four years earlier, is again on the market but is priced out of reach owing to gentrification. An extended scene in "Ebb Tide" shot in the bar frequented by the stevedores demonstrates a still vibrant culture: the place is full, there is laughter and drinking and dancing, and it is clear from casual exchanges and continual narration of tales of workplace heroism that their identities as working men are central to their sense of self. This scene, however, is intercut with shots of empty equipment and silent docks, and shots of Baltimore's closed Bethlehem Steel Plant are included in this sequence and throughout the season. Thus a sense of doomed inevitability shadows season two and viewers recognize, as Frank cannot, that his way of life has ended. Visually this is reinforced with many long establishing shots on the docks, prior to cuts to medium or close-up shots for dialogue: these long shots show machinery looming over tiny human figures, the mechanized future shown to Frank of a fully automated dock in Rotterdam ("Backwash") already prefigured in Baltimore. An important scene in "All Prologue" shows Ziggy and his father finally bonding as they walk along the docks at night, Ziggy talking about his memories of his father and uncles discussing their work crews when he was a child. Ziggy grew up wanting to emulate this ideal of manhood, but changed economic conditions meant that following in his father's footsteps was never an option. The only tender, bonding moment we see between Frank and his son is this conversation, which ends with Frank jokingly calling Ziggy "Mr. Back-in-the-Day."

By shifting its focus to the docks and by including both white and black stevedores in its casting, *The Wire* insists that these economic problems are at their core issues of class rather than race. Part of the conflict between Nat and Frank has to do with Frank's desire to extend his term of treasurer another year to finish his work on the dredging project, which goes against the informal agreement that the position should alternate between Polish and African American candidates. When Frank's involvement with smuggling is revealed and federal authorities use the investigation as a pretext to decertify the union—characters central to the drug trade having escaped arrest, as in season one—Frank's perspective seems to be validated, although his mistakes have put the union at risk (and indeed, even his bribes and lobby money have gone to waste as politicians will no longer support him once the scandal is public). *The Wire's* treatment of race is complex, and its insistence that class rather than race is the central axis of discrimination is consistent with its focus on the fuller picture of the drug culture in Baltimore.

When Nick is mourning the loss of Ziggy to prison, the anecdote he chooses to tell—which involves a prank and the punch line "college kids ain't shit" ("Storm Warnings")—further reinforces the sense that Nick and those like him resent their lack of economic opportunity. Yet Nick's refusal to see that this is something that he shares with the African Americans, whose lack of working-class tradition he disdains, is not represented with as much complexity as are other issues in the series. *The Wire* sometimes takes a false step in moving too quickly to the connections of shared class deprivation, which erases another history of systemic racism.

Multicultural Baltimore

Two facts about the specificities of Baltimore as a city are relevant here. First, the city has one of the most entrenched patterns of racially segregated neighborhoods in the United States. The politics of housing in Baltimore have long been racially charged, as is traced in detail in Anthony Pietila's *Not in My Neighborhood* (2010), and a tradition of block-busting, in which the first African American family to live on the block prompted white flight and a drop in housing values, has shaped the city such that those neighborhoods most impoverished by the drug culture and the economic shifts of global capitalism are all but exclusively African American.[1] Baltimore enacted, in 1910, "the first law in American history that prohibited blacks from moving to white residential blocks, and vice versa. When the U.S. Supreme Court seven years later struck down such laws, Baltimore again became a model that other cities copied because private agreements had barred blacks and Jews from certain neighborhoods for years" (Pietila x). Second, working-class politics in Baltimore have a long tradition of being organized by neighborhood, and thus the ethnic and religious divisions that shaped neighborhood identities were also central to class-based identities. In his study of white working-class identity in

Baltimore, Kenneth Durr is careful not simply to conflate white working-class culture with entrenched racism, but nonetheless he argues that during the economic hardships of the 1970s and beyond, the language of racism, with its politics of defense of the closed and homogenous community, was a tool that came readily to hand to a beleaguered white working class. Thus, Durr concludes, during this era "to be working class was to be white" (loc. 1189–91) in white workers' imagination.

This history informs Nick's racist comments, and indeed one might further understand the tragedy of the fall of the Polish working-class community into hopelessness as a reenactment of what happened to African American communities in previous decades. Nonwhite neighborhoods fell first because a pattern of systemic racism made them most vulnerable to the loss of work that came with the shift from industrial to financial capital. Unlike other contextual factors presented in the series, however, this history of racial politics is not directly emphasized,[2] although there are hints that writers are aware of it. In "Homecoming," when Major Colvin (Robert Wisdom) decides that the best way to minimize the damage of the drug culture is to push it toward the most unsalvageable parts of his district, he encounters a widowed African American woman still living in one of these designated neighborhoods. She is reluctant to leave and speaks with pride about her husband's tradition of manual labor and saving up to buy this house, especially because "There was some white families still living in this neighborhood then." She eventually agrees to the relocation but like Nick mourns the loss of what the neighborhood once was, questioning the priorities of an administration that has "a program that can place me somewhere else" but "ain't got no program for what's outside my door."

Similarly, in "Transitions," when drug dealer Prop Joe (Robert F. Chew) is criticized by his nephew, Cheese (Method Man), for living in an old row house despite his wealth, he responds, "Your great-grandfather was the first colored man to own his own house in Johnson Square. That means something, something you young'uns lost." Despite these comments, however, the collapse of a viable African American working-class culture is part of the distant past to the events narrated in *The Wire* and thus is not treated with the same pathos as the fall of the IBS. *The Wire*'s economic argument about the drug trade appropriately recognizes enforcement as a capitalist war on the underclass but fails to be attentive to the centrality of racial difference in this struggle. To a degree, the strong ensemble and multiracial cast suggests a postracial society, something also hinted at in conversations where, for example, Omar and Bunk reveal they went to the same high school, as is also the case for Prop Joe and police commissioner Burrell (Frankie Faison), all African American characters. Thus, it is suggested, those from similar backgrounds might equally have become cop or criminal.

39

Although *The Wire* does important work to contextualize the economics of the war on drugs, its lack of attentiveness to the long tradition of racial discrimination in Baltimore sits uncomfortably with its otherwise nuanced portrait of the community. Indeed, race is most explicitly mentioned during season three's stories of the political campaign of Tommy Carcetti (Aiden Gillen) with regard to his struggles to be elected as a white man in Baltimore. Both white and black politicians are shown to take bribes, accept drug money to advance real-estate deals, and put their careers ahead of the public they purportedly serve. The most corrupt among these, African American senator Clay Davis (Isiah Whitlock Jr.), is able to avoid prosecution for his political corruption in "React Quotes," despite overwhelming evidence that he received drug money, by disguising it as a charitable contribution. His defense, played passionately to a mostly African American jury, is that his constituents, poor black people, operate in a world outside the strictures of accountability and paper trails, in conditions of such abject poverty that the only way he might help them is by taking cash in his pockets and dispensing it as he sees fit. Defending himself during a radio interview, he suggests that he has become a target of this investigation because of his race and makes provocative comments about those willing to engage in "character assassination, tie the noose in the rope, whatever." The series is careful not to present Clay's corruption as a facet of his racial identity: white officials are equally corrupt. The district attorney who prosecutes him, Rupert Bond (Dion Graham), is African American, and Davis explicitly marks the difference between himself and Bond—and, more important, that between Bond and the jury members—as one of class, arguing "my world is strictly cash and carry," a fact invisible to "folks who never been in our neck of the woods" ("Took"). Further, it is the African American news editor Gus Haynes (Clark Johnson) who cynically describes Davis's performance as playing "not just the race card, but the whole deck" ("Took"). Finally, this story line is embedded within a number of other narratives that similarly interrogate institutional corruption and self-interest as barriers to social change, stories that implicate white as well as African American characters.

At the same time, however, the historical reality of racial discrimination makes Davis's defense compelling to many of his constituents, a truth not interrogated by *The Wire* with the same attentiveness paid to economic matters. In a telling example, the 1968 Baltimore riot is mentioned only in the context of its role in launching Spiro Agnew's national career, not as a context to better understand the jury's acquittal of Davis. When *The Wire* does raise the questions of race that haunt its stories, for the most part it does so briefly and without making the kinds of clear thematic statements that are evident regarding other issues. For example, frustrated by the lack of police resources to investigate drug killings in season five, Bunk comments, "You can go a long way in this country killing black folk, black men especially." Freamon replies, "You think if three hundred white people were killed in the city every year they wouldn't send the 82nd airborne?" ("Unconfirmed Reports"). In a season three story, Pryzbylewski is involved in a foot pursuit in alleyways and accidentally shoots an undercover black cop who is unknown to him. In the aftermath, his African American coworkers and superior support him and most believe that the racial aspect of the crime is only about surface, political appearances. Perceptively, however, a remorseful and shaken Pryzbylewski, trying to make sense of the incident, begins by saying that race did not inform his behavior, only to pause and wonder, "Or maybe it did. How the fuck do you know if that's in your head?" ("Slapstick"). *The Wire* is clearly aware that a heritage of racial discrimination and ongoing systemic racism are matters relevant to its context but less clear in its analysis than it is on other issues.

In other ways, however, the series does much to counter the pervasive association of African American cultures with criminality that predominates in media representations, particularly the ways in which it challenges more formulaic police dramas. Such earlier dramas conflated the danger attached to illicit drugs with a danger attached to the populations of the neighborhoods where the trade took place. Popular culture has played a significant role in constructing this perception. Donna Selman and Paul Leighton argue, "the news, and entertainment programs helped create the image of a typical criminal as overwhelmingly poor, black, male, increasingly drug crazed, and more and more dangerous" (loc. 804–6). Steve Macek adds that journalistic overreporting of stories on cocaine justified backlash politics against social programs directed toward inner-city neighborhoods and further established an image of inner-city residents as equally dangerous to the health of the body politic as were the drugs themselves.[3]

In blurring the boundaries between reporting and popular culture, *The Wire* brings to light the role of these media, which already shape American public consciousness, and deploys it toward counterhegemonic ends. Its revisioning of the police drama is not merely a critique of the formal limitations of this format to tell rich, contextualized stories about crime but a more direct resistance to a tradition that reinforces hegemonic attitudes toward law and order that criminalize certain populations, particularly African American ones. As Jeanette Covington argues, "One of the best strategies for making white domination appear warranted is to represent blacks as dangerous and criminal" (2). Further, since racially demarcated patterns of housing mean that whites and African Americans often do not live in the same neighborhoods, "much of what white Americans believe about blacks is based on what they can glean from movies, television dramas, newspapers, television newscasts, political campaigns, radio talk shows, blogs and other media" (20). *The Wire* is attentive to the way that the war on drugs has criminalized and further disenfranchised an economic underclass, but in its refusal to investigate fully the factors that have produced this underclass as predominantly African American, the series fails to offer a complete picture. It offers an image of criminals as complex and constrained rather than evil but fails to challenge or contextualize the popular imagination that links African Americans and the drug culture.

The Wire's representation of its criminal African Americans as rounded characters accomplishes important, antiracist work, but the series is ultimately uneven in its exploration of the consequences of racism. It succeeds more clearly in providing a context that explains crime as a response to socioeconomic and political disenfranchisement rather than as an expression of personal pathology. The degree to which the activities of the drug enterprise—even those entailing violence—are shown to be rational decisions based on a realistic assessment of one's options reduces the sense of absolute distance between a "them" engaged in the drug trade and an "us" of legitimate society that has previously dominated. Season three's story of Colvin's program to provide what he calls a "paper bag" solution to the drug problem enacts arguments that Simon and Burns make in their book *The Corner* about the need to understand drugs as a problem of public health rather than one of criminality.[4] Such arguments are similarly premised on a refusal to conflate those who use and deal drugs with the dangers represented by the drugs themselves. Upset by one of his officers being shot in what he regards as strategically useless hand-to-hand surveillance busts, Colvin announces the next morning at roll call that they will cease the policing strategy of arresting low-level drug crews and instead will push the drug trade to targeted zones where enforcement will not be a priority. This solution reflects the reality that their enforcement strategies only relocate the drug trade anyway, and they gain from this new plan an agreement that there will be no violence. Further, Colvin wants to remove the problems associated with drug traffic and addicts from the rest of his district to free officers to follow up on robberies and other investigations, "the kind of police work that is actually worth the effort, that is worth actually taking a bullet for" ("Time After Time").

This strategy produces a neighborhood dubbed Hamsterdam that, while the doomed experiment lasts, accomplishes these goals, as is made evident by frequent shots of peaceful neighborhood streets with women hanging laundry, children playing, and other scenes of quotidian peace. Similar shots of Hamsterdam show a community of great poverty and suffering: teenagers no longer serve as lookouts for the drug corners left without task or money; drug addicts overdose unnoticed in the corners of abandoned buildings; sex takes place in the alleys; and shambling human beings hollowed out by their addiction crowd the streets. Based on intervention from Deacon (Melvin Williams), however, Colvin begins to address some of these issues with help from community organizations dedicated to AIDS prevention, addiction treatment, and other public health services, and is even praised for making accessible an at-risk community generally too elusive to treat. Once the project is revealed to the media, even the mayor briefly considers whether it can be salvaged before the federal government steps in and makes clear that they regard this experiment as a legalization of drugs and hence ideologically anathema. When Hamsterdam is finally dismantled in a massive police raid in "Mission Accomplished," police cars roll in and armed officers round up drug dealers and drug addicts alike while Wagner's "Ride of the Valkyries" blares from police speakers. Angela Anderson notes that the war on drugs was used by federal administrations in the 1960s and 1970s "partially as an excuse to integrate federal power with local policing," and more particularly that these policing powers were targeted at controlling particular populations: the poor and nonwhite whose neighborhoods were most vulnerable to the economic and escapist promises of drugs. *The Wire's* depiction of this war on drugs as a war on the underclass is made inescapably clear in this sequence, which depicts the police as an occupying army.

The ruins of bulldozed Hamsterdam.

Neoliberal Drug Trafficking

The Wire is able to make visible the links between capitalist economies and the drug trade by highlighting the absence of other economic opportunities in inner-city neighborhoods. David Wilson argues that since the 1990s a new kind of ghetto has been produced in the "rust belt" cities of the United States (of which Baltimore is one). Real-estate development interests benefit from narratives of inner-city recovery that pathologize neighborhoods conflated with the drug culture, and as Macek notes, the neighborhoods most affected by gentrification projects were also, owing to historical segregation and ongoing discrimination, most likely to be African American. Wilson argues such spaces are "understood around a new debilitating theme of hopelessly pathological and destructively 'consumptive' [spaces]" (loc. 229–34), represented as a drain on needed tax dollars and an impediment to newly minted gentrification plans that were touted as the solution to these cities' struggling economies and a necessary response to the competitive world of globalization. He calls these new spaces "the glocal ghetto" (loc. 172) and argues that the stigma attached to their residents in popular and political representations "is currently a key ingredient to controlling and confining this population; managing people in the neoliberal era is as much done by producing stigma as construction and implementation of rules and regulations" (loc. 2633). In adding complexity to its presentation of those involved in the Baltimore drug trade, *The Wire* resists this stigmatization and returns our attention to other social and economic forces that have isolated and deprived such communities.

The centrality of drug organizations to economic life in isolated and impoverished inner cities has been documented extensively by Sudhir Venkatesh. He links the rising role of criminal gangs in the lives of many young men in Chicago (a city with much in common with Baltimore in terms of migration and employment) directly to the same economic forces analyzed by Wilson. It was only in the 1970s that people began "looking to the gang to make money; in part, this was an expected response, given unemployment rates for youth that hovered around 50 percent in Chicago's ghettos" (*Off the Books* 66). Venkatesh calls the new gang structure a "corporate gang" (282) and argues that it emerged to fill two needs in the lives of African Americans confined to the projects. It provided economic opportunities for those otherwise marginalized by racism and a shrinking labor base, and enabled them to achieve the prestige denied by their inability to move into "municipal and corporate boardrooms" (*American Project* loc. 837–41), spaces newly opened up to middle-class African Americans by civil rights victories. Studying the unemployed and impoverished youth culture in Los Angeles in the 1980s, Mike Davis notes that the rise of financial capital left young people with no options other than a "crypto-Keynesian youth employment program operated by the cocaine cartels" (309). The lives of many characters echo this lived experience.

The Wire explores these parallels, especially by contrasting Avon Barksdale, his lieutenant Stringer Bell, and Marlo Stanfield, who controls the drug trade by the end of the series. Avon represents a connection to an early stage of "the game" through inheriting his father's drug empire. Although he is clearly motivated by profit and has little concern for the effects of his business on the addicts, he nonetheless remains connected to and part of the community (a pattern Venkatesh observes in his history of drug trafficking in Chicago). Avon respects those who want to leave "the game" and represents a model of capitalism that is consistent with the Keynesian era, in which there was a sense of a social contract between labor and capital. In "Middle Ground," for example, he gives $15,000 to Dennis "Cutty" Wise (Eugene R. Little), once a drug enforcer who finds he is unable to return to this life of violence after he is released from a fourteen-year prison sentence, to fund the gym Cutty establishes for street youth. In Avon's drug world the system remains exploitative, but there is a social safety net and human social relations persist beneath the commodity exchange. We see Avon participate in a community barbeque and a later a basketball game, and in his discussions with D'Angelo he stresses the importance of family and love as part of their enterprise. Yet Avon is also willing to be brutal when necessary, as is demonstrated in season one when he orders the torture and murder of Brandon (Michael Kevin Darnall), Omar's lover, in retaliation for the robbery of their stash house. In "Cleaning Up," when advised by his lawyer to ensure that no one is in a position to hurt him, he authorizes the murder of Wallace, who has been talking to the police.

Wallace's murder produces a break between Avon and D'Angelo, leading D'Angelo to reject his uncle's discourse of love, arguing "they playing you with their 'we family and it's all love.' When they got no more use for you that family shit disappears and it's all about business" ("Undertow"). The reality is more complicated, however, and although Avon makes a number of choices to kill those close to him—even acquiescing after the fact in the murder of D'Angelo—he is always represented as torn by these decisions, trapped in a system that compels him to act in such ways. When Brianna (Michael Hyatt), D'Angelo's mother, convinces him that he cannot betray his uncle by entering witness protection but instead must serve his jail term for the sake of his family, she stresses to D'Angelo that it is only the economic drug enterprise that allows them to exist: "This right here is part of the game, D, and without the game this whole family would be down in the terrace living on scraps. Shit, we probably wouldn't even be a family" ("Sentencing"). For Avon, the drug enterprise is a necessary business and one that requires him to sacrifice others at times, but it is also a part of his identity in a way that is similar to the pride Nick expresses in his stevedore heritage. Avon fought to win control over the project towers, a lucrative site of drug distribution,

47

and he angrily resists Stringer's attempts to give up some of that territory. Later, when the projects are demolished, Avon goes to war with Marlo over control of the most lucrative street corners and insists on the importance of his reputation in seizing them. The kind of drug culture that Avon represents thus, in some ways, parallels the Fordist moment of capital that is nostalgically evoked in Frank's efforts to dredge the docks and ensure the future of manual labor.

Stringer, in contrast, constantly seeks financial security above all else and strives to make the drug trade parallel, as much as is possible, the legitimate world of capitalism. He introduces a cooperative partnership among Baltimore drug dealers and pushes for the resolution of issues in the boardroom rather than with guns. While Avon is imprisoned, Stringer begins to use Roberts' Rules of Order in meetings, trying to educate corner dealers in the different marketing techniques required for inelastic and elastic products that he has learned in his community college economics classes Stringer is not nostalgic for an earlier mode of production and does not see social as well as economic relationships in his dealings. He founds the New Day Co-Op to get the best price on drug shipments through a cooperative arrangement to share both product and territory, and increasingly is more interested in stock market and real-estate deals than in the drug enterprise. In season three he begins to wear suits and frequently meets with politicians and developers, a world that clearly bores Avon. Stringer even insists that they run their copying shop "Like a true fucking business. Not no front, not no bullshit" ("One Arrest"), although it is indeed precisely that. In "Homecoming," he tries to talk Avon out of a war over corners with Marlo, insisting that it will only bring the police and reduce profits. His language—"It ain't like it was. You ain't got to pay no price to buy no corners"—represents the growing gulf between them, as Avon is quick to note in his incredulous response, "Since when do we buy corners? We *take* corners." In a later conversation, this contrast is linked to their

Stringer in business class.

different attitudes toward life in the ghetto: Avon reveals that he never expected to live into his thirties, whereas Stringer plans escape to a life of legitimate businesses founded with money from the drug trade.

"Middle Ground"

The polarization between Avon and Stringer and the larger questions of possibility for reform of inner cities to which they point are made clear in the season three episode "Middle Ground," written by George Pelecanos and directed by Joe Chappelle. As with all episodes of *The Wire,* this one advances a number of different plotlines in ways not always evident in the absence of the full text, a tendency even more apparent in this mid-third-season episode. "Middle Ground" begins with a confrontation between Omar and Brother Mouzone (Michael Potts), a character whose bow-tie ensemble, intellectual manner, and quip that "the most dangerous thing in America" is "a nigger with a library card" ("Storm Warnings") echo Malcolm X (beyond these surface allusions, Mouzone's politics are never developed). Both characters are well-known to audiences by this point: Omar as a charismatic outlaw and Mouzone as a New York enforcer crucial to the conflict between Avon and Stringer. The scene builds on such prior knowledge, particularly of an earlier event in which Stringer misled Omar to pit him against Mouzone: no meaningful dialogue is exchanged between the two characters; they face one another with guns drawn from opposite ends of an alley, each embodying his distinctive personal style. We learn later in the episode that crucial information is exchanged in this encounter, and then we learn it only by inference. Skilled readers of the show are able to understand that Stringer's duplicity was revealed in this encounter, but casual viewers may struggle to understand. The pleasures in this scene are derived from its atmosphere as these two iconic characters face off against one another in a manner reminiscent of westerns and as they exchange witty barbs in their distinctive idioms. Omar's dialogue even evokes the cadences of the western: "I keeps one in the chamber, in case you pondering."

After the credits we cut to another showdown of sorts, as Stringer consults their lawyer, Maurice Levy (Michael Kostroff), about the real-estate applications he has made under the corporate name B&B Enterprises and learns that the bribes he has paid to Clay Davis have bought him nothing. Stringer is confronted with the fact that his college education did not prepare him for the duplicity of the "game" of capitalism, and he is mocked by Levy; they sit on a bench in an interior courtyard, and through the arch of the entryway we can see a legislative building in the distance, filmed in an upward tilt that emphasizes the degree to which Stringer remains trapped in the small, cave-like setting of his world while the brightly lit legislative building looms over him in the distance. Later scenes stress

Omar and Mouzone face off.

that Stringer is isolated and cut off, not only from the world of finance to which he aspires but also from the street he strives to leave behind: we cut to a warehouse in which Avon and his crew are gathering weapons, planning a full assault on Marlo. They are dressed in jeans or tracksuits, lounging comfortably Stringer is stiffly out of place in his suit, angrily pacing as he demands that a "hit" be put on Clay Davis. Slim (Anwar Glover) calmly responds, "Murder ain't no thing, but this here some assassination shit," provoking Stringer to an even angrier insistence that his orders be obeyed.

Stringer is marginalized figuratively in this shot as the camera looks over the sitting Slim's shoulder and through the doorway, where Avon stands listening. He enters the room and walks to stand beside Slim, leaving Stringer alone on the opposite side of the desk. Like Levy in the earlier scene, Avon mocks Stringer's naiveté in believing he could enter this other world. The camera stays with Avon as it watches Stringer angrily stride away, Avon calling after him, "They saw your ghetto ass coming from miles away." The next shot of Stringer shows him alone in his office at the copying shop, looking through his development paperwork and becoming increasingly frustrated, until we finally see him swap the chip in his cell phone and go outside to make a call. Our perspective then cuts to the surveillance detail watching him on the screen: we can see that he is talking but cannot hear what he says. As with the opening shot of Omar and Mouzone, the significant dialogue (Stringer is reporting Avon's parole violation to have him arrested and end the unprofitable war) is implied here by the configuration of actors and the audience's presumed knowledge of previous events. This conflict between Stringer and Avon is the main

focus of the episode, and it culminates in a mutual betrayal, their two conversations intercutting with one another: in one, Stringer meets Colvin in a cemetery and reveals the location of the war room; in the other, Avon obliquely discusses Stringer's hit on Mouzone, ultimately reaching the conclusion that the only way he can continue his drug enterprise is by letting Mouzone take revenge.

In each conversation, the issue of loyalty versus business is raised. Stringer tells Colvin that he trusted him with this information because he saw Colvin's attempts at reform in Hamsterdam. Colvin insists that there must be more to the story than Stringer is revealing, that for Stringer to be willing to give up a man he calls brother, "He must have done something to you," but Stringer demurs, "Nah, it's just business." In contrast, as Avon talks to Mouzone and tries to offer money to compensate for the "mistake," he is told, "Business is where you are now, but what got you here is your word and your reputation. With that alone you still have an open line to New York; without it, you're done." Drawing upon the western ethos of individualism that shapes the aesthetic of the opening sequence, this exchange suggests a romanticized view of the drug trade as Avon participates in it, where reputation has meaning and there is something that might be called honor among thieves. These intercut scenes are also played as tragedy, each conversation composed of shot and countershot close-ups of the faces of the participants, with long pauses on Avon and Stringer as they make their final decision to betray the other, their expressions conveying sadness and regret as well as capitulation.

For those who know the entire series, however, the nobility of Avon's gesture is particularly futile. The New York connection he was at such pains to protect fails him in the next season, leaving him vulnerable in the emerging war with Marlo. Understood within this larger context, Avon's nostalgia for an older version of the drug trade is even more naïve than Stringer's belief that he could become legitimate, reminiscent, in fact, of Frank's faith that dredging the canal will save the working-class culture of stevedores. This scene is also an example of *The Wire*'s problematic negotiation of the tension between narrative impact and social realism. In writing the scene of Avon and Stringer's mutual betrayal as a kind of high tragedy, the series privileges fate over the agency of two African American men. Allowing the narrative demands of tragedy and dramatic irony to dominate the sequences has the tendency to naturalize such individuals as doomed to abject fates, shaped by their circumstances to "naturally" betray each other. The thematic emphasis on the damaging, deterministic, and pervasive force of capital becomes elided here, through dramatic staging, with a more impersonal and universal forces of fate, thereby not only construing these lives as hopeless but also undermining the more pointed economic critique.

The personal tragedy of Avon and Stringer's mutual betrayal is further paralleled in this episode by scenes that mark the inevitable defeat of Colvin's project to make the drug trade less destructive. Other scenes show Carcetti confronting Colvin with his knowledge of the experiment and asking for his side of the story. The audience, with Carcetti, gets a tour of the good,

53

the bad, and the ugly: we see neighborhoods safe once again for children to ride bikes and for neighbors to visit on stoops; police are able to demonstrate more arrests on non-drug-related crime because their resources are no longer futilely used to lock up addicts and street-level dealers; and a community meeting includes a woman extolling the benefits of a neighborhood in which she once again knows her beat cop and he her. When the car pulls up to Hamsterdam, the establishing shot shows people stumbling across streets, drugs being openly sold, and a few police standing idly by to prevent violence. We cut to a profile shot of Carcetti and Colvin talking in the car. Colvin explains that he will leave Carcetti to complete the remainder of the tour alone, announcing, "I ain't claiming no kind of victory" but also that he is nonetheless glad he tried to do something different. He then sends Carcetti to walk through the neighborhood alone with the promise, "What you're gonna see ain't pretty, but it's safe."

This exchange illuminates an earlier scene in which Carcetti and Colvin stood on a street corner across from an old funeral home and Colvin told him a joke about its previous owner's response to desegregation: when asked if he was now going to bury black people, Colvin explains, this white man responded, "Yes, if I can do them all at once." Carcetti looks uncomfortable while Colvin laughs uproariously before pausing to explain that he has a degree of respect for the funeral parlor owner because one always knew where he stood. In telling this joke just before taking Carcetti to see Hamsterdam, knowing that Carcetti's political power could either support or further undermine his experiment, Colvin implies that the current regime of drug enforcement is itself a racist policy that, like the fictional funeral parlor owner, seeks to bury "black folks" all at once but fails to admit its desire to do so. In such moments, the series most directly reveals its indebtedness to literary fiction and its challenges to the episodic format of previous television.

Two more scenes in "Middle Ground" are particularly worthy of note. The first is the extremely emotional final exchange between Avon and Stringer, who share drinks on Avon's balcony overlooking the city. By this time, each has betrayed the other. The scene begins with a medium shot of both from behind, showing the city lights in the distance, as they try simply to enjoy one another's company but inevitably fall into an argument about whether they should go to war with Marlo. Looking out over the harbor, they remember their youth of poverty and share an anecdote about Stringer stealing a badminton set and being chased by a security guard. As Avon reminds him, this was a ridiculous theft because they did not have a yard, but it is clear from their further exchanges that it was the middle-class lifestyle embodied in this item that motivated Stringer. They allude briefly to 1970s civil rights struggles—something not significantly developed, consistent with the series' truncated ability to engage seriously with the politics of race.[5] Avon notes that Stringer aspired to own two grocery stores, while he wanted an AK-47. This sequence is written with dramatic irony, the audience knowing more than each individual character, and the dialogue is both small talk and symbolism as each character says good-bye: Avon asks Stringer to stay with him and dream a bit about the journey they took to arrive at this height; Stringer insists, "We ain't got to dream no more, man, we got real shit, here to stay, to touch." Although they are in the same shot for much of the scene, the characters look away from rather than toward one another, failing to connect physically just as they do in dialogue. Final close-ups on their faces, over one another's shoulders in a final embrace, capture their conflicted emotions, but neither attempts to change the events they have set in motion.

The next day Omar and Mouzone confront Stringer at his development site. Demonstrating his familiarity with the gangster life he has previously disparaged, he reacts quickly to the threat of violence and runs. He is followed by Omar, who slowly and methodically paces behind him, and is finally

Stringer and Avon talk of the past.

stopped by Mouzone, who is sitting on the stairs leading to the top floor. Stringer once again insists that he is no longer involved in that "gangster bullshit" and offers them money to let him live. Inevitably, given their characterization as motivated by ideals, not money, they refuse. Finally realizing his death is inevitable, Stringer shouts, "Well, get on with it motherfuckers!" before being riddled with bullets and falling before a large window. Omar and Mouzone briefly stand looking down at Stringer and then walk out of shot as the camera stays with the body and slowly tilts to show the billboard through the window proudly proclaiming, "New Real Estate Opportunities Coming Here Soon, Brought to You by B&B Enterprises." The episode's final image is a medium-long shot of Stringer's body before the window with this sign visible through it. *The Wire* refuses to glamorize the violence it depicts: despite many murders over its sixty episodes, few shots focus on the gore of wounds. Choosing to kill Stringer at this building site rather than a location associated with the drug trade suggests that the two enterprises are equally destructive of the lives of the impoverished residents in the cities in which they flourish. Had he succeeded as a developer, Stringer would have been responsible for just as much pain and poverty as he would have if he had remained in the drug business alone.

In this episode, *The Wire* demonstrates its willingness to kill a major character. Given that Stringer is killed by popular characters whose claim to justice is stronger than his own, his death is not presented with the same level of tragedy as attended the death of, for example, Frank in season two. This death also continues the series' work of undermining the conventional investigative narrative because it prevents police from capitalizing on the wiretap recording of Stringer discussing drugs, which

Stringer dies in front of his dream.

was the police's major breakthrough earlier in this episode. In the following episode, as police search Stringer's apartment, McNulty pulls Adam Smith's *The Wealth of Nations* from the shelf, finding this evidence of intellectual pursuit, as well the apartment's restrained decor, inconsistent with his image of a drug dealer. Thus Stringer's narrative complicates viewers' understanding of the drug trade and the motivation of individuals within it, directly countering the stereotype of the crazed black psychopath critiqued by Macek and Covington. Although Stringer's financial ambition is directly linked to his downfall, the complexities of other aspects of the series do not allow this scene to be read simply as a rejection of African American aspiration: rather, the real tragedy of Stringer's death is linked to his limited opportunities, making the drug trade his only avenue toward the legitimate economy. Venkatesh makes a similar argument about the necessity of the underground economy for those living in Chicago's ghettos, criminal and "citizen" alike: "Without a change in the kinds of resources that make their way into places like Marquis Park, there will never be much in the way of meaningful opportunities for inner-city inhabitants to experience economic stability—let alone upward social mobility" (*Off the Books* 387).

Further, Stringer's intense focus on profit over other factors is openly critiqued. In his efforts to make the drug trade more closely parallel the legitimate economy and his valuing of profit above all else, Stringer embodies a harsher logic associated with Reaganomics and the dismantling of the welfare state. Stringer does not let sentiment stand in the way of business decisions, even if at times he still feels it. He thus sets the stage for the even more predatory, neoliberalist mode of drug trafficking personified by Marlo, whom we never see have personal relationships. Marlo's one sexual encounter is with a woman sent by Avon to set him up, and when he later learns of her complicity he waits for her at her home and shoots her, twice in the chest and once in the head. It is significant that he does this killing personally:

both Avon and Stringer have killed in the past, it is implied, but we do not see them directly engage in violence in the series. The first time Marlo appears on screen, a drug addict, Johnny (Leo Fitzpatrick), lets a shopping cart crash into the side of his vehicle, and one of Marlo's enforcers puts a gun to Johnny's head and threatens him as Marlo comes out. Clearly looking bored and lacking any concern with the morality of killing a man over a scratched vehicle, Marlo says in an even tone, "Do it or don't, but I got someplace to be" ("Time After Time"). Marlo lacks affect, conveying a sense of menace through the absolute flatness of his manner and tone. He kills people much more readily than did Avon, including his own people, and we rarely see him engage in any but the most pragmatic conversations. Marlo is the face of capitalism stripped of any value other than profit: he kills an entire family based on a challenge to his street credibility and would rather kill and replace expendable workers than risk having them compromise him. Indeed, Marlo behaves as a sociopath in his absolute disregard of anything other than his own desires and the bottom line, suggesting the characterization of capitalism as itself sociopathic, as seen in the documentary *The Corporation* (Ackbar and Abbott, 2003). He is even compared directly to Wal-Mart in "Late Editions" for sending a crewmember disabled by a gunshot to jail in place of the real culprit, who remains able-bodied and thus useful to Marlo.

Marlo's more predatory mode of capitalism is dominant by the series' end: he has forced the Barksdale crew into working for him or retiring, and Avon is no longer able to support the families of those of his crew in prison, in much the same way as the bankruptcies of corporations eliminate not only jobs but also pensions. Further, Marlo dominates the Co-Op in the manner of a hostile takeover, willing to accept whatever benefits can be gained from cooperation but balking when asked to accept his share of any losses, quickly ready to turn to violence if it will serve his ends. Joe educates Marlo in "the game" beyond the street level, teaching him how to launder his money and

Marlo—a more predatory approach.

avoid wiretaps, and yet when Marlo sees the chance to take over Joe's operation and control the entire city, he does not hesitate. He gains access to Joe's home by providing favors—against the explicit directions of the Co-Op—to Cheese, a disaffected employee at this point. When Marlo comes to kill him, Joe protests, "I treated you like a son." Marlo calmly replies, without affect, "I wasn't meant to play the son." Marlo embodies the single-minded pursuit of rational self-interest that is the ideal of *homo economicus* in marketing models. Once he controls drug distribution for the entire city, he immediately raises the price for street-level dealers. When one complains that he cannot sell at a competitive rate given this higher price, Marlo proposes that the dealer simply extract more surplus value from those below him; faced with further objections to this failure to respect the social contract between dealer and employees, Marlo merely shrugs and says, "Short yourself then." Profit exists for him in a world divorced from social context.

Yet despite his economic success, Marlo remains like Avon in that the street is all he knows, and he loses his sense of identity without it. In one of his least sympathetic acts, Marlo goes to a corner store, buys water, and then overtly steals a lollipop in full view of the security guard. This man follows him outside to confront him, careful to insist that he is not "stepping to" Marlo but that he nonetheless feels Marlo should show some respect for the fact that this man is there, working at a dead-end job for minimum wage, simply to support his family. Rather than feel any sense of solidarity with someone trying to survive the same economic conditions he has escaped, Marlo shows only contempt for this man, and in a later scene we learn that the security guard has been killed for talking back to Marlo when Snoop casually throws away his badge.

For Marlo, being part of a community is not even conceivable and, unlike both Stringer and Avon, he does not understand the drug enterprise as a way to escape the poverty he otherwise faces but merely as a normalized activity, one at which he happens to excel. Thus, although he has an opportunity to succeed in the move to legitimate profit from finance capital and development that motivated Stringer, Marlo walks away from this opportunity and instead returns to the violence of the streets.[6] As he has insisted in earlier conversations, his entire identity is defined by wearing "the crown" ("Homecoming") as top drug dealer in the city. Although this character effectively embodies a shift in the structures of capital toward more openly exploitative forms that match contemporary shifts in capitalism itself, part of what achieves this effect is that Marlo himself is as empty and faceless as the forces he represents. Thus, unlike Avon and Stringer, he does not emerge as a full human being but more as a symbol of—perhaps on an individual level the product of—the broken social systems of inner-city poverty.

61

The System Is Broken

Look, they gonna tear this building down, they gonna build up some new shit. But people? They don't give a fuck about people.

63

Bodie Broadus, "Time After Time"

The pursuit of profits over people, and of career advancement over substantive results, is one of the series' themes, and its effect is traced across a number of parallel institutions: the police department, the drug-trafficking organization, political governance structures, the school system, and the media. *The Wire* shows the common dysfunction across these locations, systems in which those with power use it to protect their own interests and those without are victims of structures they can neither perceive nor resist. *The Wire* demonstrates the way that neoliberalism's colonization of social life creates a context for public service in which performance statistics dominate over any other criterion of job performance, even when those statistics demonstrably do not reflect meaningful results. Police officers, school administrators, and politicians work to manipulate the system to serve their own ends, just like drug dealers. Season two ends with the dissolution of the union, which has been charged with corruption: federal prosecutors have no interest in pursuing the trafficking in women and drugs, but are interested only in prosecuting waterfront corruption and removing the union as a political obstacle. In season three, Colvin loses his job as a consequence of Hamsterdam after being demoted so that he also loses a larger pension, and the stigma prevents him from being hired as security guard at Johns Hopkins University, which was to have been his post-police work. As in most of The Wire's story lines, those who challenge the status quo and work for systemic change are punished and disempowered while those who think only of their own advancement prosper.

The police department is the most obvious target of this theme of institutional failure, and, as I have already argued, one of the most significant ways that The Wire revises the police drama format is in its refusal to depict the closing of cases, even if there are arrests, as victories for justice. The entwined problems of crime and poverty have systemic causes and can only be addressed by systemic solutions. Not only does the series repeatedly dramatize the fact that arrests do not substantively change anything, but at times it further suggests that police intervention actually makes things worse in the absence of other, more encompassing solutions. For example, the progress Cutty makes with troubled youth in his gym during season three (the advent of Hamsterdam means they are not needed as lookouts anymore) is mostly undone when the neighborhood is razed and they return to the street corners—although a minor glimmer of hope remains in the brief appearances of Justin (Justin Burley), among the more troubled of his students, still in the gym in the subsequent season and in the example of Cutty, who is able to build a life beyond the drug trade. When Avon is arrested a second time at the end of season three, this clears the way for Marlo's unchallenged dominance, creating an even more predatory culture. Repeatedly we are shown the inefficacy of a police department that cares more about protecting people's careers than about protecting the communities it is meant to serve. The most significant results it produces, ironically, are Carcetti's election to mayor (based on a scandal regarding a witness shooting that is later proven to be accidental) and later to governor (based on the press coverage of the serial killer faked by McNulty and Freamon).

The first season constructs parallels between the drug enterprise and the police department, often through intercut scenes, demonstrating that in each those lower in the hierarchy must find ways to accommodate the at-times capricious demands of those above and reinforcing a sense that the drug enterprise is, from the point of view of many involved, merely employment. In each site, numbers drive goals, seemingly a reasonable expectation for a sales enterprise like the drug trade but one that hinders legitimate investigative work when applied to the police department. *The Wire* shares with *Homicide* the focus on "the board" where murders appear in black or red, designating closed or open cases, with the clearance rate used to evaluate detectives.[1] In *Homicide,* the board was treated as an expression of ego, the pressure to have only black under one's name one of the characteristics of the familiar crusading, heroic cop; in *The Wire,* its institutional function is underscored, and detectives must battle superiors who want the clearance rate made favorable by whatever means necessary (including "dumping" murders on other agencies, arresting on charges they know will not hold in court, or prevailing upon medical examiners to "downgrade" murders to accidents). Investigations that reveal unreported crimes (thus challenging the clearance rate) or that require long and costly surveillance are disparaged in favor of superficial ones that provide the instant gratification of improved arrest statistics while leaving untouched the systemic causes of crime.

This failure to understand problems as systemic and thus to craft appropriate solutions is one of the chief targets of *The Wire's* satire as its extends its vision of failed institutions to incorporate politics (which plays to entrenched beliefs to gain votes), education (pretending children are progressing to ensure continued funding), and finally the media (which is critiqued for pandering to Pulitzer juries who prefer pathos to substantive analysis). In each case, *The Wire* reveals that activities undertaken to generate a certain statistical outcome will not only fail to achieve their purported aim but will prevent any meaningful and systemic change. The stories concerning the electoral process and the educational system in seasons three and four make this claim most directly. The upcoming election puts extra pressure on the police department to ensure that crime statistics make the current administration appear competent, which leads to ridiculous exchanges such as Mayor Royce (Glynn Turman) insisting that he was promised a murder rate of "275 or under" ("Homecoming"), as if statistics could compel material reality to match their prescriptions (less humorously, police majors are relieved of their command and replaced for failing to bring in the desired numbers). Similarly, the mandatory state school test categorizes most of the students as proficient, which a veteran teacher explains to an astonished newcomer means they are reading at two grades below their level. The systemic problems that Carcetti sought to address when he began his mayoral campaign soon become only so many statistics (crime rates, test scores, voter polls) that he must manipulate in order to pave his way to a governorship, and in one of the most depressing yet realistic scenarios he refuses to accept $50,000 of state money desperately needed by city schools because this would hurt his county vote. He rationalizes that he can better help the city as governor but later agrees to give away half of any monies he raises as governor to another county in order to compel a rival candidate to drop out of the race.

Although *The Wire* presents this systemic failure of institutions as a pervasive aspect of life in late capitalism, crucially it never loses sight of the specificity of Baltimore as a contingent location. As has been noted by critics as well as by the actors in

DVD commentary, the city itself is the main character, linking the disparate people, locations, and themes of its five seasons. As Linda Speidel argues, *The Wire* uses its establishing shots neither to provide a recognizable postcard skyline nor to create a vision of Baltimore as uniformly dangerous and menacing. Rather, such shots produce Baltimore "as a lived environment," a use of space that refuses to represent the drug corners or the Pit as "an anonymous crime scene" but shows them as simultaneously "a place where ordinary life goes on." Frequently the crime scenes themselves contribute to the social critique of institutions that have abandoned the inner city to poverty and decay, such as frequent shots of block upon block of abandoned row houses that form the backdrop to many scenes in season four, a technique that relies on the audience's knowledge—prior to the detectives'—that the bodies of Marlo's victims are hidden in such properties. When the investigation finally discerns a pattern in the use of nails rather than screws to board up these houses, the sheer number of vacant homes in Baltimore overwhelms investigative resources. In season five, *The Wire* similarly films investigators exploring the spaces under bridges, alleyways, and other sites where the homeless congregate, using the investigation to bring to the television screen parts of American urban life frequently invisible or represented simply as nightmarish and alien spaces. In *The Wire,* the abandoned houses contain both bodies and children squatting and making do as best they can without resources; the bridge tunnels are inhabited by both the schizophrenic homeless and displaced families carefully scrubbing clothing on a washboard.

Bodie Broadus

David Harvey, drawing on Marx and Engels, notes that large cities are a manifestation of capitalist social organization and that the problems of nineteenth-century cities, predominantly sanitation and epidemics, are sites of risk in which the pathologies the elite visit on the working class threaten to spread to the capitalist classes themselves. Thus were born various strategies for organizing and segregating urban space by class and designs to reduce mobility between impoverished and wealthy neighborhoods, all to ensure that stigmatized people and their pathogens remained in the ghetto. Harvey notes, "Today it is social pathology—drugs and crime—which is important, but the problem does not seem essentially different" (142). *The Wire* makes such false divisions manifest, such as in a scene in "Old Cases" where McNulty, running late for his children's soccer game, drives to the suburbs with drug addict informant Bubbles, who queries, "Where in leave-it-to-Beaver-land are you taking me?" The city occupied by McNulty's ex-wife and his children is physically contiguous with but ideologically disconnected from life in the inner city. This utter social divide is encapsulated in the language employed by those "in the game," which includes the addicts, to distinguish themselves from the rest of the city's denizens, whom they call taxpayers or citizens. Most crucially, we are shown that what truly drives the drug culture is the money it funnels to politicians and developers (whose political influence ensures that they will never be prosecuted for their role in impoverishing inner-city neighborhoods), indeed often to those whose activities are not technically criminal although clearly implicated in the larger network of which the drug trade is a part. In this critique of institutions and systemic privilege, *The Wire* demonstrates the cost at the individual, human level of the limited opportunities available to those within marginalized neighborhoods. By tracing the lives of characters across several seasons, the series reveals consequences of the drug trade that could not be conveyed as effectively by a more episodic narrative structure, as is suggested by the character Bodie Broadus.

Bodie is an ambitious and hardened young man who quickly embraces the realities of the world he is given and seeks to use his innate intelligence to succeed. He keeps his head in challenging situations and thinks about strategy as he works his drug corner. In season one, Bodie is also particularly brutal and largely unsympathetic, especially when compared to D'Angelo, for whom he serves as foil. In the first episode, "The Target," he participates in a brutal beating of an addict who attempted to scam them for ten dollars and scoffs at D'Angelo's compassion. In "The Buys" he punches an alcoholic policeman during a raid and is himself severely beaten by police; he later simply walks out of the juvenile detention facility. This initiative gains Stringer's attention and Bodie is later selected to murder Wallace, a crucial moment for his commitment to the corner lifestyle. Bodie, Poot, and Wallace all grew up together, and when they are given the order to kill Wallace, Poot hesitates and questions if it is necessary. Bodie insists that they must act because "the man says so . . . the man gave the word," and thus they are faced with a choice: "We either step up or we step the fuck off . . . that's the game." Poot and Bodie kill Wallace in "Cleaning Up," an action that serves as their initiation into the adulthood of their community: Bodie effectively distances himself from the killing by challenging Wallace's ability to be a man instead of a boy, claiming, "You's a weak ass nigger man . . . you brought this on yourself." Wallace's "weakness" has earlier been linked to his compassion: he cares for a number of neighborhood children, all of whom live with him in an abandoned house without adults—a quality that links him with D'Angelo and makes them both unsuitable for the drug game. Bodie and Poot hesitate before shooting Wallace, but both follow through in the end; they are both approximately sixteen at the time.

Despite such inauspicious beginnings, we are given reasons to like Bodie as the series progresses and to understand his hardness as a product of his social circumstances rather than an expression of his innate nature. In "Ebb Tide," he believes the radio is broken as he loses reception to a Baltimore station on the drive to Philadelphia for the new drug supply, marveling, "The radio in Philly is different?": this scene demonstrates to viewers the very limited horizon in which Bodie lives and makes choices. Yet despite this naïveté, he is quick to see through rhetoric, refusing, for example, to reminisce nostalgically about the project towers when they are leveled at the beginning of season three, the fate of most low-income housing in rust-belt cities in the early twenty-first century. While Poot recalls important personal experiences lived in the towers, Bodie realizes that their real loss is a site of revenue: "You live in the projects, you ain't shit, but you selling dope up there you got the world by the ass." He is one of the few Barksdale crew not arrested at the end of season three because he is smart enough to claim that the Hamsterdam experiment was entrapment. Much later, in season four's "Final Grades," he is taken by McNulty to eat lunch on the stately grounds of Baltimore's Cylburn Arboretum, the public park surrounding an 1863 mansion, and expresses shock that they are still in the city. Despite the degree of financial security that the drug trade has given him, Bodie literally lives in a different America than that occupied by the middle and privileged classes. His intelligence and work ethic ensure that he survives longer than Wallace or D'Angelo, both of whom are hampered by their empathy, but ultimately Bodie, too, is doomed by the limited prospects of inner-city life.

By season four, Bodie, now approximately twenty years old, begins to realize that the game is stacked in favor of those who already have power. After building up his own drug corner as an independent, following the collapse of the Barksdale organization, Bodie is compelled to work for Marlo. He complains bitterly to Slim that things are not like they were in the old days of working for Avon ("Home Rooms"), but Slim, too, has had to accommodate himself to new workplace realities and now works for Prop Joe. In *The Wire*'s paralleling of institutions, Bodie's situation matches that of employees faced with the choice of working for inadequate wages in poor conditions or being unemployed because no viable economic alternatives remain.[2] Bodie reaches his breaking point in season four when Marlo kills one of his crew, Little Kevin (Tyrell Baker), on suspicion of snitching. Bodie is aware that this suspicion is ungrounded and furthermore was the one to insist that Kevin explain himself to Marlo rather than allow rumors to put him at risk. When Kevin's body is found in an abandoned row house, Bodie lashes out, exclaiming, "This motherfucker be killing niggers just to do it. This motherfucker be killing niggers just because he can. Not 'cause they snitching, not 'cause its business, just because this shit just comes natural to him. . . . This motherfucker don't feel nothing. And all those niggers in the row houses don't mean a thing to him." Bodie had been able to rationalize a certain amount of violence as inevitably part of the drug trade while working for the Barksdales, and indeed was even willing to enact it, but he also believed in the Barksdale enterprise as analogous to a family, once again evoking the parallel to a Fordist compromise between management and labor. Poot argues that Marlo's killing of Little Kevin is no different from their own murder of Wallace, but Bodie insists that Marlo has crossed a line; the balance has shifted too far in favor of those with power who no longer recognize and reward loyalty.

Bodie refuses to accommodate himself to this neoliberalist logic of unregulated capitalism. Marlo is the embodiment of this ethos in the drug trade, and Bodie's resistance to profit without human restraint leads him to consider helping the police, although he is adamant that he will not implicate any Barksdale people or others he feels play "the game" according to appropriate rules. He explains to McNulty,

> I've been doing this a long time. I ain't never said nothing to no cop. [Pause for reaction shot.] I feel old. I been out there since I was thirteen and I ain't never fucked up the count, never stole off a package, never did some shit that I wasn't told to do. I been straight up, but what come back? You think if I get jammed up on some shit they be like "Alright, yeah, Bodie been there, Bodie hang tough. We got his pay lawyer, we got his bail." They want me to

stand with them, right, but where the fuck is they at when they supposed to be standing by us? I mean when shit goes bad and there's hell to pay, where they at? [Another long pause.] This game is rigged, man. We be like the little bitches on the chess board.

As Bodie begins the monologue, we see a medium shot of him and McNulty on opposite ends of a park bench. As it continues, the camera focuses on his face, one of the most frequent shots used by *The Wire* for delivering significant dialogue. Bodie rarely meets McNulty's eyes and seems to be talking to himself as much as to McNulty. After this monologue, he identifies his caveats and then offers his assessment while looking directly at McNulty and saying, "Marlo, this nigger and his kind, man, they gotta fall, they gotta." McNulty and Bodie exchange a few more words before the camera cuts to a long and high shot

McNulty and Bodie discuss the game.

of them on the bench, dwarfed by the surrounding park. This scene is one of the most effective for demonstrating both the complexity and the humanity of a character who in season one seemed a caricature of a thug and further reinforces *The Wire's* argument that the drug culture must be understood as an economic system, one that parallels not only the profits but also the exploitative flaws of capitalism. Before the episode ends, Bodie has been killed on his corner, refusing to run although he knows his death is inevitable. The centrality of this minor character's story to the major themes of the series—as well as the emotional scenes written to dramatize his turning point and death—demonstrates that in *The Wire* "all the pieces matter," as Freamon says of their investigation in the season one episode "The Wire."

Bodie's tragic life and death anticipate the central theme of season four: the prospects for children in inner-city neighborhoods who grow up with the drug trade as their horizon of expectation. Kraniauskas describes the show as following "an accretive looping logic that incorporates *more and more* of the social (through its institutions)" (26) but critiques it for failing to follow this logic through the chain of money and political corruption, returning instead to the street and the story of how boys end up on the corner. I would contend instead that this returned focus to what is visible on the corner is consistent with *The Wire's* themes. The failure of the school system and other social programs has produced individuals who are out of reach of the local police; this refusal to follow the money also demonstrates a reality of contemporary capitalism, "the opacity of accumulation and circulation . . . so that it is possible to capture *that* we are tragically enmeshed in the urbanised accumulation and reproduction of capitalism through its territorially specific institutions but it is exceedingly difficult to define *how* this takes place" (Toscano and Kinkle). Our inability to visualize the complex intertwining of legitimate and illegitimate finance, to understand how the same people who refuse to fund social pro-

Bodie dies defending his corner.

grams are those funding gentrification that is further marginalizing the poor, is at least contested by *The Wire*. Season four traces the fate of four fourteen-year-old boys, Randy (Maestro Harrell), Namond (Julito McCullum), Dukie (Jermaine Crawford), and Michael (Tristan Wilds), from the end of the summer and through the school year, as they find their various fates in the corner neighborhood.

"Final Grades"

A central plotline concerns an innovative program for at-risk youth funded by a sociologist from Johns Hopkins University (Dan DeLuca) that seeks to separate troubled students from regular classrooms and provide them with training that will help them negotiate the social spaces of their classrooms and the world beyond the corners, environments for which their experience has not prepared them. The rationale is that this program will remove their disruptive presence, which will facilitate learning for the rest of the students, and prepare the troubled students to rejoin regular classroom study. Despite measurable successes, it is stopped partway through the year and all classes are mandated to prepare for the standardized state test, part of President George Bush's No Child Left Behind program. Rooted in a market ideology that claims to reward results, this program ties school funding and administrator bonuses to test performance, thus putting pressure on these institutions to teach to the test rather than address their students' educational and other needs. Typical of neoliberal policies, this structure funnels resources to those already advantaged and further penalizes schools struggling with poverty and students whose lives have been disrupted by the drug war. When he is told that the youth program has been canceled because the school cannot allow social tracking, Colvin, who was recruited post-retirement as an advisor for the program, insists, "We're leaving them behind anyway" ("Final Grades"), and can only laugh when the professor feels that a published study that informs further studies is sufficient achievement.

"Final Grades," written by David Simon and directed by Ernest Dickerson, dramatizes that those most in need are not served by institutions whose mandate is to help them. As a season finale, it demonstrates even more strongly than the other episodes discussed thus far the cumulative logic of *The Wire*. Without exception, the most significant scenes achieve their meaning based on the audience's knowledge of events in earlier episodes, demonstrating the rich and multilayered quality of *The Wire*'s narrative and even anticipating motifs to be developed in the season that follows. This episode, like many, includes scenes that provide pleasures of double meaning: in one, an exchange between McNulty and Daniels about proper investigative techniques (quick, street-level arrests versus long, wiretap investigations) directly repeats dialogue from season one but with the speakers reversed. In its first iteration, McNulty angrily denounces Daniels; in the repetition, Daniels repeats the same lines back to McNulty tongue-in-cheek, obliquely commenting on the friendship that has grown over the previous seasons and the changed attitudes toward police work each has developed as a result.

The season's story arc is a bildungsroman of sorts, and this episode represents the movement of each of the four boys into the adulthood available to them and, with one exception, represents a closing down of possibility from the potential embodied in the boys they once were. Each episode of *The Wire* begins with a tagline, generally of dialogue that will appear later in the episode, a pithy statement that encapsulates the episode's key idea: "Final Grades" begins with the tagline, "If animal trapped, call 410-844-6286," the notice that appears on plywood boarding up abandoned row houses (and, attentive viewers might recall, the number Poot instructed a girlfriend to call to ensure Wallace's body was discovered in season one). The school that was the setting for many of season four's important scenes is no longer prominent in "Final Grades," and indeed the first school to appear onscreen in this episode is not that middle school but a closed high school whose gym has become the staging area for the bodies taken from the vacant homes. The first shot is high and wide angle, capturing in a single frame the twenty-two sheet-covered corpses lined up in neat rows. Assistant DA Rhonda Pearlman (Deidre Lovejoy) is explaining the status of the investigation to Daniels and Deputy of Operations Rawls (John Doman): there are fifteen thousand vacant homes in the city and thus more bodies might arrive, and although they have gathered trace evidence from each scene they have no budget to process it. Thus the finale begins with an investigation instead of wrapping up this season's case.

The most significant events of this episode concern story lines other than this murder investigation. The scene of Bodie's death is significant in the development not only of his character

The vacants—casualties of drugs and capitalism.

but also of that of Michael, the most independent and toughest of the young boys. Over the course of the season, we learn that Michael is the primary caregiver to his younger brother, their mother lost to drug addition to such an extent that she sells their food to gain her fix. Michael works briefly for Bodie before school starts, but he refuses the handouts of money Marlo offers to neighborhood children to gain their loyalty. His self-reliance provokes Marlo's interest, and over the course of the season Michael is torn between his resistance to obligation and his inability to resolve the problem presented by the return of a sexually abusive stepfather. Michael, more skilled at fighting and other kinds of violence than his peers, cringes when approached by this man and eventually capitulates to accepting help from Marlo's enforcer Chris (Gbenga Akinnagbe), which entails also agreeing to train as an enforcer. It is Michael who shoots Bodie, walking up behind him and without hesitation firing two bullets into his head. Murdering Bodie marks Michael's first independent kill and his entry into "the game." The camera zooms in on Bodie's face for this scene (and significantly does not focus on the gun or the wound), whereas Michael's face is hidden by the shadow of his hood, rendering him almost anonymous, reinforcing the erasure of Michael's specific identity—his capacity for playfulness, generosity, and kindness seen over the season. As Bodie falls to the ground, his hood falls across his face as well, allowing the camera to pause and hold on Bodie's body as the audience grieves his loss but refusing to display his fatal wound as spectacle.

Dukie is the most vulnerable of the boys and the one with the most academic potential. His significant scenes in this episode do not include any dialogue, emphasizing his increasing isolation and portending a dire future (by the end of the series, he has become a drug addict). In his first scene, a long shot shows Dukie walking up the block to his home, the shot centered on the pile of the family's belonging outside the door; in a later shot, he approaches the door of his middle school but turns away before he reaches it. In both scenes, Dukie's isolation is emphasized. We have learned from earlier episodes that his family are drug addicts who regularly sell his belongings and that he lives without running water or even a change of clothes. Under the guidance of a caring teacher, the former police officer Pryzbylewski, Dukie has proven to be compassionate and intelligent, a child who might flourish in a more stable environment; on the streets, however, his lack of aggression dooms him. Now cut off from his middle school by social promotion, he has also lost the one relationship with an adult that gave him a vision of a world beyond the drug corner. A later scene in the home he moves into with Michael continues to emphasize Dukie's isolation: he enters alone and walks upstairs; through a crack in the doorway he sees Michael having sex with a girl; Dukie pauses and watches for a few beats, then hangs his head and walks into another bedroom where he checks on Michael's sleeping little brother; he tucks the blanket more firmly around the child and then walks alone to his own bedroom where he sits with his head in his hands, listening to the thumping sex from the next room. Scenes such as these show *The Wire's* deep investment in characterization and the attention given to themes that have little to do with the police investigation but everything to do with the larger context that produces drug crimes.

Randy becomes caught up in the murder investigation when police investigate his repetition of rumors about Little Kevin's death and he is labeled a snitch. Consistent with Marlo's ruthlessness, he demands retaliation even though Randy has no actual information that could hurt Marlo. Randy is ostracized and attacked at school, and later his home is set on fire, severely injuring his foster mother and leaving him homeless. In the final season Randy, a friendly and open child who flourished under his foster mother's care, becomes hardened and suspicious in the changed social setting of the group home he is sent to after her injury. In "Final Grades," hints of this transition are apparent in the sequence of Sergeant Carver (Seth Gilliam) transferring Randy to this home. The sequence opens with an establishing shot that begins at the top of the group home and tracks down the door where Carver and Randy get out of the car: Randy's last moments of childhood openness are captured in a close-up on his face as he says, "It's okay, you tried," and taps Carver's arm before he walks in (Carver went to extraordinary lengths to avoid this moment, including offering to foster Randy himself, but systemic rules prevented such intervention). The scene cuts to a shot from high on top of the stairs inside the building, looking down on a tiny Randy as he begins to climb them, Carver trailing reluctantly and far behind. As Randy enters the room he is to share with five other boys, the camera pans across their resentful faces, then cuts to a medium shot in which he is all but obscured by their larger bodies.

The sequence ends, however, not with Randy but with a cut to a shot outside of Carver walking back to the car. He gets in and the camera stays outside, filming him through the window as he gives in to his rage and grief (he feels responsible for passing the boy's name on to a police colleague who carelessly revealed it to Marlo). Through the glass, we see Carver shouting and punching the steering wheel, the only sound the beeps of the car horn. The sequence ends with a long pause of his face as he blinks back tears. Within the context of watching this episode, this sequence contributes to the pathos *The Wire* articulates surrounding the fate of corner boys in inner-city neighborhoods; within the series as a whole, however, this sequence is important also for what it reveals about Carver, a character who changes over the series from just one of many cops interested in the adrenalin rush of their work to someone committed to serving the community he polices.

Aspects of this transition are visible in season three as he supports Colvin's experiment with Hamsterdam, in contrast to Sergeant "Herc" Hauk (Dominick Lombardozzi), who sees tolerating drug use as a betrayal of the values of law and order that brought him to the police department. It is Herc who put Randy at risk and who eventually reports Hamsterdam to the press. The contrast between Herc and Carver, partners in season one and distinctly different by season five, is further evidence of the way *The Wire* rewrites the conventions of police drama. Herc represents the values associated with the tough-on-crime vision of the 1990s, while Carver represents a less militant mode of policing, something closer to the friendly and compassionate officers of earlier series such as *Adam 12* (NBC 1968–75) but informed by a much grittier and more complex vision of the social world in which policing takes place. Although the series rarely draws attention to this fact, it may also be significant that Carver is African American while Herc is white and thus perhaps more willing to criminalize the predominantly African American neighborhoods associated with the drug trade.[3]

The most interesting plotline in "Final Grades" concerns Namond, the son of Wee-Bey, who is pushed into the drug trade by his mother throughout the season and who fails to acquire the necessary hardness for this life. Colvin comes to know Namond through his work with the special school program, and Carver takes an interest in Namond because of his shifting attitude toward policing. Both are distressed by the dismissive attitude Namond's mother, De'Londa (Sandi McCree), shows toward her son's fears of violence and jail, prompting Colvin to approach the jailed Wee-Bey and offer to adopt Namond. Their conversation encapsulates the series' thesis that the drug trade is becoming worse and more predatory. Colvin tells Wee-Bey that Namond is "smart and funny and open-hearted" and has the capacity to be anything he wants to be but that he will not survive into a meaningful adulthood if he says on the corners: "People in the game nowadays, it's a whole different breed: no code, no family, damn sure no respect."[4] Here *The Wire* again suggests that the drug trade is merely a kind of work available to those in impoverished neighborhoods: Wee-Bey's realization that the world has changed and that it is not viable for Namond to follow in his footsteps reminds us of Frank's similar realization about Ziggy and the docks in season two.

Wee-Bey agrees, and the final sequence of the episode shows Namond, the only one of his peers to end the season with his childhood intact, doing homework on Colvin's porch. From within we hear Colvin's wife calling him to bring in the plate from his snack. One of his friends from the corner, Donut (Nathan Corbett), drives up in a stolen car, and he and Namond share a nod before Donut drives off. The camera follows the car as it speeds away, heading toward downtown, which we see in the distance; Namond is now safely isolated from that world by several blocks of peaceful streets. In a more conventional drama, this happy resolution to Namond's story might be the moral center of the story, a tale of success despite tragic circumstances. Everything else about *The Wire,* however, has trained viewers not to invest in such consolations. Indeed, Beliveau and Bolf-Beliveau point out the sinister fact that Namond's very success is also "the confirmation of middle class values, which in some ways are the very historical and material source of the inequalities inflicted on the poor" (103). While we may feel relieved that Namond was saved from the fate that generally awaits boys like him, his rosier future is made possible only by the most fragile of contingencies, and such individualistic solutions—like individual arrests—do nothing to change the systemic problems of poverty and crime.

Media, Social Justice, Community

I'm not interested in what can be quoted.
I'm interested in what feels true.
Gus Haynes, "Took"

T*he Wire*'s claim to significance is based on its commitment
to social realism and its willingness to tell a "truth" about
crime and justice that is obscured by both other popular culture
and mainstream discourses about crime. In this final chapter, I
want to consider *The Wire*'s relationship to its audience and the
question of whether its nuanced depiction of the drug culture
is simply sophisticated entertainment or can achieve something
more substantial in the relationship between world and text.
Further, I want to examine *The Wire*'s unique relationship to
the Baltimore it depicts, not only in terms of the way that the
city figures as an important character in the drama but also in
its insistence of filming Baltimore *in Baltimore*, employing both
local actors and local residents.

Fan and critical response to the show is split as to the question of whether it inspires social change or further exploits the
lives of marginalized people by turning them into entertainment. In an exchange published in *Dissent* in the summer of

2008, John Atlas and Peter Dreier contend that *The Wire* was too cynical in showing only the negative side of inner-city poverty: its bleak vision of poverty, they feel, contributed to an image of inner-city citizens as helpless and hence works against social change. As I argue above, this problem emerges from the tension between *The Wire*'s journalistic/documentary ambitions and its reliance on narrative precursors that privilege fate over agency. Anmol Chaddha, William Julius Wilson, and Venkatesh, in contrast, argue that although they respect the achievement of Baltimore activist groups celebrated in Atlas and Dreier's account, they nonetheless feel that such efforts were "insufficient counterweights to entrenched structural forces, when . . . a deepening crisis continues to mark ghetto neighborhoods across the United States" (83). Fan response to the show is a significant and developing phenomenon that requires further research, a task made challenging by the online format of much of this commentary and the difficulty of ascertaining the identity behind screen names. Nonetheless, there seems to be some evidence that fans connect their responses to the show with their assessments about crime and poverty beyond the series. Kathleen LeBesco's preliminary study of responses to the character of Omar Little on HBO's official series bulletin board concludes that at the very least *The Wire* provokes serious discussion of criminality, violence, drugs, and homosexuality, even if it is difficult to ascertain the social class of the participants in such conversations.

Audience and Agency

One of the concerns raised about the program is that it is voyeuristic, representing a population unlikely to be among its viewers. Yet there is some evidence that a wide range of social classes view *The Wire*. Ventaktesh's blog "What Do Real Thugs Think of *The Wire*?" published on Freakonomics (http://

freakonomics.blogs.nytimes.com/) in 2008 recounts his experience of viewing and discussing the program with Chicago gang members. Further, Hua Hsu notes that a gang recently arrested in New York claimed that they had learned from the series to avoid police investigations by frequently switching their cell phones (509). Although it seems unlikely that the social classes depicted on *The Wire* are the bulk of its audience given its circulation on subscription channel or DVD, I would also argue that the middle classes are more urgently in need of the perspective it offers. As Freamon observes in "Unconfirmed Reports," "A case like this, where you show who gets paid, behind all the tragedy and the fraud, where you show how the money routes itself, [reveals] how we're all, all of us vested, all of us complicit."

The series' role in documenting the complexity of the drug war and its economic sources with compassion and understanding brings to American television a tradition of social realism and public service that has informed production in Canada and the UK. Yet *The Wire*'s existence on HBO means that its market position is distinct from these public service commitments. A show such as *The Wire* seems able to thrive only in the conditions created by the shift toward subscription channels not beholden to public or advertising funds. Indeed, the complexity of its narrative suggests its format is viable only in such contexts, in which viewers approach television with the attentiveness previously reserved for film, as is suggested by the recent cancellation of *Detroit 1-8-7* (ABC 2010), a network police drama that embodied some of the qualities of *The Wire* in its multiracial, ensemble cast and episodes that linked the investigation to specifics of the city. In "*The Wire*'s War on the Drug War," Burns, Lehane, Pelecanos, Price, and Simon answer the question of what one might do in response to the social world made visible by *The Wire*. They propose resisting complicity in class war by refusing to reach guilty verdicts for nonviolent drug offenses on juries, asking people to "think for a moment on Bubbles or Bodie or Wallace. And remember that the lives being held in the balance aren't fictional."

In a letter to fans published on HBO's website in 2008, Simon laments, "we seek simple solutions. We enjoy being provoked and titillated, but resist the rigorous, painstaking examination of issues that might, in the end, bring us to the point of recognizing our problems, which is the essential first step to solving any of them." *The Wire* is committed to political analysis and change, what Simon calls, in his letter, "non-fiction truthtelling," and in part it achieves this effect by its careful blending of real life and fiction, drawing equally on the powers of documentary implicit in some of its casting and story choice, if not in its aesthetics, and on the power of the naturalist fiction. Yet at the same time *The Wire* also provides titillation and enjoyment, praised for characterization and narratives rather than for political intervention. However, it is not easy to construct a simple binary between "real" life and fiction when it comes to *The Wire*. Many extras are local residents, often referred to casting agent Pat Moran by their parole officers through a connection to former police officer Burns. Many of the actors were recruited from the local Baltimore theater scene, most prominently Robert F. Chew, who plays Prop Joe. As Lisa Kelly notes, "The often impenetrable accents and highly specific colloquial vernacular make no concessions to the average viewer but instead demand their attention and commitment"; this is another way that the show both connotes realism and compels viewers to pay attention to people they normally do not see. The ubiquity of so-called reality shows on network television is also relevant to the intervention accomplished by *The Wire*. Such programs push the boundaries of what might be called reality in scripting and editing of raw footage into contrived scenarios, and a reality show such as *Cops* (1989–) is guilty, like failed journalism or tough-on-crime police dramas, of constructing an oversimplified view of criminality that is countered by *The Wire*.

Cast and crew choices demonstrate a commitment to the people whose lives are represented by the series. The production team included Fran Boyd, a former drug addict central to Simon and Burns' *The Corner,* as well as her two sons, DeAndre McCullough (who also appeared as the character Lamar) and DeRodd Hearns. Fran's partner, Donnie Andrews, a former stick-up boy whose life was a partial inspiration for Omar (Alvarez 296), worked in production and appeared as a version of himself onscreen. Tyreeka Freamon, the mother of DeAndre's son and an important figure in *The Corner,* appeared in minor roles and worked on production. As well, prominent figures in Baltimore make cameo appearances, most significantly former mayor Kurt Schmoke, whose argument that drugs should be considered a decriminalized health problem led to him being labeled "the most dangerous man in America" by New York representative Charles B. Rangel (Alvarez 278). The recurring character of Deacon is played by Melvin Williams, a former drug dealer who is the model for Avon Barksdale and was employed on *The Wire* when he was released from prison. Felicia Pearson, for whom the show temporarily served as a way to leave the corner, plays Snoop. As she explains in her memoir *Grace after Midnight* (2007), she found that "by showing my reality, these motherfuckers are changing my reality. . . . The only way to leave my fucked-up reality is to throw myself into the pretend version of my fucked-up reality. . . . *The Wire* is throwing light on that darkness. That's what the show's about" (225). Unfortunately, despite a number of years free from the drug trade, Pearson pleaded guilty to drug-related charges in August 2011. Her story, like that of Namond discussed earlier, emphasizes that any possible change is limited to isolated cases and is dependent upon contingencies subject to change again. In the absence of the employment provided by the show's production,

87

she once again found herself with few economic opportunities. The systemic change the show calls for is a trickier matter but perhaps not entirely out of reach. Angela Anderson argues that *The Wire* is not about presenting solutions to the social problems it depicts but rather that "The resolution is elsewhere, in the residue of affect that lingers long after the television is turned off, and in the viewers' relationship to the characters, which is an empathetic relationship exactly because the characters are flawed, ambiguous and contradictory figures."

This quality of melodrama in the series, which encourages us to identify with and care about the characters, is at least as important as its commitment to realism. While it is important that *The Wire* embodies Baltimore and its people in both themes and material production, the power the show holds over its viewers comes from its qualities as well-written and well-acted fictional drama. Writing is obviously crucial to the show's meaning and success, but the power of the professional actors to bring these figures meaningfully to life should not be underestimated. Nowhere is this truer than in the character of Omar Little, played by Michael K. Williams. Unlike many characters, Omar is infused with the powers of fiction: he becomes a legend for his fearlessness and style within the diegesis as much as among viewers without. Williams's chiseled good looks enhance his charisma, made only more intriguing by the real scar that bisects his face from forehead to chin. From his initial appearances Omar challenges viewers' preconceptions about gangsters: he is openly gay and the greater freedoms of HBO allow him to display this affection sexually. He has a distinctive, almost poetic cadence of speech, never curses—unlike most characters—and soon becomes known for his iconic presence as he strides about the neighborhood in a long black duster, hiding beneath it his signature shotgun.

Omar is a mythic figure in this otherwise gritty drama: he insists upon his own moral code, which excludes violence against those he calls citizens, choosing to rob only those in the game. He refuses to distribute drugs as a business, rejecting the way the drug culture preys upon a desperate community (he does sell drugs he steals to other dealers, making this a compromised stance at best). In one of his first scenes, he offers drugs for free to a woman who is clearly suffering from withdrawal, an act that is presented as compassionate ("Old Cases"). In his most compelling performance in "All Prologue," Omar serves as a witness against a Barksdale enforcer in the murder trial: he wears the necktie the prosecutor insisted upon around his neck like a scarf and—unlike other characters in *The Wire* and in typical police drama representations of drug dealers in courtrooms—he refuses to mimic middle-class comportment and speech, instead maintaining his own relaxed manner and distinctive way of speaking. When asked to identify his occupation, he casually responds, "I robs drug dealers," and when challenged by the defense attorney, Levy, as to why the jury should believe the testimony of a convicted criminal, he merely shrugs and says, "That's up to y'all."

In his courtroom behavior, Omar's openness and honesty—not equivocating about his arrest record or making excuses for his violent behavior—encapsulate the humanization of the criminal that is the larger project of *The Wire,* and he wins over the jury just as he does series viewers. He becomes intense only when Levy accuses him of violent crimes no different from the one at hand: Omar insists there is a difference, that he "ain't never put [his] gun on no citizen." He is most effective as Levy continues, "You are feeding off the violence and the despair of the drug trade . . . stealing from those who are themselves stealing the lifeblood of our city." Interrupting the attorney's oration, Omar interjects, "Just like you, man," stunning Levy into silence as Omar observes, "I got the shotgun. You got the briefcase." Omar then shrugs as he concludes, "It's all in the game, though, right?" From here Omar's status as a figure untainted by the drug culture around him grows, indeed to such an extent that writers felt compelled to write a scenario

Omar becomes an iconic figure.

to counter the degree to which some viewers glamorized him, a popularity that worked against the grain of the show's otherwise unromanticized portrait of the drug trade.[1]

In a crucial scene, Tosha (Edwina Findley), one of Omar's robbery crew, is killed during an attempt on a drug stash, and Omar, talking with Bunk, who is investigating the crime, argues that it should not be a priority for the police, that it was all part of "the game" with "no taxpayers . . . no victim even to speak of" involved ("Homecoming"). Bunk rejects this logic, angrily insisting that Omar's moral dichotomy oversimplifies reality, that Tosha had a family who mourns her and that the real crime is an attitude that writes off part of its citizenry as "in the game" and hence no longer subject to the same moral universe. Echoing Colvin's comments about the changed rules of this game as its logic colonized and displaced all other aspects of life in certain neighborhoods, Bunk talks about his memories of being a young man in the same school as Omar attended and being told by older boys not to become involved in the street violence: "As rough as that neighborhood could be, we had us a community. No body, no victim, it didn't matter. And now all we got is bodies and predatory motherfuckers like you. And now where that girl fell I saw kids acting like Omar, calling you by name and glorifying your ass. Makes me sick, motherfucker, how far we done fell." Omar's response lends weight to Bunk's critique and, for a time, he retires from the game, reentering it only for reasons of personal vengeance in the final season in scenes that enhance his role as a vigilante hero motivated by values greater than money and thus allowing narrative priorities to undermine social critique.

It is only in Omar's death scene in "Clarifications" that *The Wire* retreats from this heroic myth. In the previous episode Omar escaped being killed by Marlo's enforcers by jumping from an improbable height over a balcony, an unrealistic outcome that was, in Marlo's words, "some Spider-man shit" ("Took"). In the next episode, the injured Omar attacks another drug corner without incident, throwing away their supply and repeating his mantra that Marlo is "not a man for this town" before entering a corner grocery to buy a pack of cigarettes. In a scene absolutely without dramatic tension, the camera shows a close-up on Omar's face as he hears the bell of someone entering, glances briefly to the doorway, and then returns his focus straight ahead toward the position of the clerk. Without warning we hear a pop and see a brief slash of red, and then his body disappears from view as he drops to the floor. The scene cuts to the murderer, the child Kenard (Thuliso Dingwall), standing in the doorway clutching a gun and looking frightened, filmed from a low angle as he hesitantly approaches the body, then drops the gun and runs away. Despite Omar's heroic status throughout the series, his death is presented in a very low-key sequence, undermining at last the glamour of being a stick-up boy. What's more, we later learn that his death is not significant enough to warrant inclusion in the newspaper. In the episode's final sequence, a morgue clerk examining two side-by-side bodies, one Omar's and the other a middle-aged white man, eventually decides, based on their names, that their identification tags have been misplaced and switches them, followed by a close-up of Omar's face as the zipper closes the body bag over it in his final appearance onscreen.

Through this emphasis on Omar's largely unnoticed death, *The Wire* draws attention to a gap between the priorities of its narrative world (and presumably of its fans) and those of the material world outside the drama, which is otherwise oblivious to the lives of those in the drug trade. In this way, the series draws viewers' attention to the difference in their own experience of intense loss at the death of Omar as compared to the absence of concern—even of stories—about lives such as his, an absence that would not previously have even registered as

Omar's minimalist death scene.

such. At the same time, however, the centrality of Omar to the overall narrative in his role as a figure who critiques and fights against worse predators such as Marlo points to the crucial importance of techniques of fiction, not those of documentary realism, to *The Wire*'s achievements. His popularity and narrative power are indicative of *The Wire*'s accomplishments as text, an aspect of the series that can sometimes disappear from view in the praise given to its themes of social critique as a representation of what is true and real. I contend that the series' commitment to producing good-quality drama blunts its goals of social critique at times because the narrative requirements of tragedy belie the possibilities for social transformation that are also part of Baltimore. *The Wire* does important critical work in deconstructing the simplistic narrative closure characteristic of law-and-order police drama, but in its unwavering focus on the rigidity and totalizing effects of institutions, it at times errs in emphasizing structure over agency too much.

93

Women of the Wire

Although most of *The Wire*'s departures from strictly documentary realism are thoughtful and used, such as this characterization of Omar, to clear thematic ends, in one significant respect the series fails to fully capture or comment on social reality: its depiction of gender. There are few women on *The Wire*—and few involved behind the scenes in writing and directing—and in stark contrast to the series' ability to depict complex matters with nuance in most other areas, its gendered stereotypes are predictable and formulaic. In part, its masculine bias can be explained by the environments it depicts: both police work and the drug trade statistically involve more men than women; as well, consistent with HBO's use of sexual titillation as one of its trademarks, *The Wire* sets scenes in strip clubs or brothels as one way to provide a context for onscreen female nudity. (To its credit, *The Wire* also includes full frontal male nudity, albeit in a nonsexualized context, something dared by few other series.) Yet at other times *The Wire* seems merely unreflectively to mirror a misogynistic culture often endemic to such locations, such as an extended conversation about masturbation between Landsman (Delany Williams) and Rawls in season one's "Old Cases" that serves as the slightest of pretexts to introduce a discussion of McNulty's problems with authority.

During a 2005 public forum at the Museum of Television and Radio about the series, included in the season three DVD extras, an African American woman in the audience challenges the cast and writers about a scene in which D'Angelo is confronted during an interrogation with gruesome crime scene photos; his female, African American district attorney (DA) visibly flinches when she sees them. This audience member, identifying herself as a DA from Detroit, insists this response is unrealistic and mars what she otherwise takes to be an accurate portrayal of the reality she knows. The unsatisfactory response she receives is that the scene was about D'Angelo's guilt and the DA's reaction was necessary to establish an outside moral perspective. This is an example of both privileging narrative over social realism and failing to develop rounded female characters. A fictional show is expected to privilege the needs of characterization and theme over realism and so from one point of view this choice makes sense; at the same time, however, given that creator discourse on *The Wire* insists on the accuracy and "truth" of its representation, casually violating the commitment to realism to achieve narrative effects is problematic. While *The Wire* is a television milestone for its achievement in deploying the police drama form to the ends of social critique, it is an uneven accomplishment and remains troubled by the tension between entertaining drama and social realism.

Narcotics detective Kima Greggs (Sonja Sohn) comes closest to being a female lead, and *The Wire*'s struggles to imagine a confident and powerful woman are revealed by making her a lesbian—which the series seems to imagine as a female man, even showing her growing similarity to McNulty—and by suggesting, although not explicitly claiming, that her sexuality explains why she is tougher than most female cops. When she comes out to McNulty in "The Buys," their conversation almost immediately shifts to a discussion of how she had her "ass kicked once or twice" and realized "it is not the end of the world" and so found her confidence for the streets. *The Wire* refuses to sensationalize as mere spectacle Kima's female relationship with her partner, Cheryl (Melanie Nicholls-King), however, and stories focusing on them parallel stories about male characters: their growing distance over Cheryl's resentment of Kima's job is explicitly connected with Daniels's deteriorating marriage in a sequence of intercut, icy dinner scenes in their respective homes in "Hard Cases," and she and Cheryl eventually break up when Kima follows too closely in McNulty's footsteps and begins cheating. Assistant DA Rhonda Pearlman is the only other female character that shares significant screen time with the male actors, and although she is not depicted in a pejorative way she nonetheless lacks the complex interiority of most of the major male characters. She is initially involved in an affair with McNulty that contributes to the breakup of his marriage, and although she complains about his failure to provide for her emotional needs, she nonetheless continues to have sex with him for most of the first two seasons. Further, a judge's infatuation with her helps them obtain crucial warrants and other legal assistance, implying that her sexuality matters along with her legal expertise.

Other minor female characters suggest that the writers tried to address the difficulties with female characterization: D'Angelo's mother is defined by her concern for him but nonetheless pushes him into accepting a drug charge to protect the family enterprise; port police officer Beadie Russell (Amy Ryan) struggles to keep up with the murder case in season two but quickly rises to the challenge and becomes a valuable if minor member of the team; political analyst Theresa D'Agostina

95

(Brandy Burre) intellectually dwarfs those around her and even McNulty desires to pursue a more meaningful relationship with her, her casual attitude toward their sexual encounters making him feel that he's "just a breathing machine for my fucking dick" ("Reformation"). As with Kima's character, however, the strength of Theresa's character comes from patterning her on traditionally masculine traits. This is also mirrored in Snoop, the only female character with any prominence in the drug trade, who is all but indistinguishable from her male partner, Chris. Although such characterization does suggest a vision that imagines women can be good at roles otherwise stereotypically imagined as male ones, the representation nonetheless remains problematic in the show's overall lack of interest in its female characters as rounded individuals. Further, these women do not get as much screen time as do the men. Courtenay Marshall sees progress from the typical depictions of women in crime dramas in some of these figures, suggesting that characters such as Brianna allow black female participation in crime in ways other than prostitution, while those such as Shardene (Wendy Grantham), a stripper who briefly serves as a police informant, allow us to see "fallen" women as complicated characters: Shardene does not treat stripping as anything other than a source of income and, when given the opportunity to leave this life, she goes to school to train to be a nurse.

Yet despite such positive moments, *The Wire's* treatment of gender is simplistic. There are a number of minor female characters who are depicted in very negative terms without any context to explain how their circumstances have contributed to character: Dukie's and Michael's mothers both appear only as drug addicts willing to prey on their own children; De'Londa more aggressively pushes Namond into drug dealing to ensure her own material comfort, scorning the concern expressed by Carver and Colvin; Daniels's wife, Marla (Maria Broom), berates him for his lack of ambition and withdraws her affections when he refuses to put his career before his principles; finally, both she and his new lover, Rhonda, compel him to give up a promotion in order to protect secrets that might damage their respective careers. Carcetti's wife, shown to be a model of sweetness and support throughout his campaign, demurely says, "You'll do the right thing," when he tries to talk to her about his dilemma with school money, thus failing to develop as a character with her own reasons for being involved in the political process and missing a narrative opportunity for Carcetti to be confronted with his failing ideals. *The Wire* is certainly not the only police drama to fail to write compelling roles for female characters;[2] nonetheless, this is a disappointing limitation of a series that is otherwise so careful to capture the complexity of a mode of life. The series' overall social realism is compromised by its failure to be as attentive to female experience.

No Second Acts

This issue of how and why one represents social issues becomes not only an organizing principle for *The Wire* but also the central issue within its diegesis in the final season when attention shifts to the city newspaper. In some ways, this final season is the weakest because its central characters are distant from the world richly imagined in the previous seasons. This very distance, however, is the point as *The Wire* pulls back from intensive focus on Baltimore drug corners and explores why most of us were unaware of these realities, just as the reporters within the series are oblivious to this dimension of their city. Leigh La Berge reads this shift as a metafictional one through which "psychological, serial violence [of the fake serial killer] both critiques and undercuts the series' realism by self-consciously moving the narrative from following the exchange of money to create representation to now following the sale of representation for money" (558). Many of the stories in this season parallel the work done by *The Wire,* demonstrating that this television series and journalism both use techniques drawn from documentary and fiction and, further, that the now dominant standards in journalism result in "factual" reporting that is less accurate than the "fiction" of *The Wire.* For example, the editor calls Scott Templeton's (Thomas McCarthy) story on an inner-city boy who wants to attend the Orioles opening game a portrait of "the disparity of the two worlds of this city in a highly readable narrative" ("Unconfirmed Reports"). That Templeton has fabricated this boy is only part of the satiric point: more important, this *kind* of story, a small and affective anecdote that allows its audience to visualize the aspirations of inner-city youth without confronting a systemic need for change, is what is valued by the press. This, Simon maintains, is precisely the problem, as he explains in an interview with Andrew Ryan: "all the problems of the American city depicted in the first four seasons won't be solved until the depth of those problems is acknowledged. And that won't happen without an intelligent, aggressive and well-funded press."

Episodes throughout season five stress the need for newspapers to tell the complex truth about our social reality, not merely to reduce stories to questions of individual pathos, as Templeton does with the baseball narrative, or to sensationalize stories to make incidents and events seem more exciting, as Templeton later does in a story about an Iraq War veteran. *The Wire* rejects the kind of narrative described by fictional *Sun* executive editor James Whiting (Sam Freed) as "the tragedy of a forgotten world, the Dickensian aspect" ("Late Editions"), this adjective seeming to mean, in this context, as removed from the reality of the paper's readers as are the tragedies of the nineteenth century. Yet Dickens, like *The Wire,* used detailed social realism linked to stories of charismatic individuals to depict and critique the failings of his contemporary society and in other contexts is one of the precursors to whom Simon points.

The series, then, partakes of this creative molding of truth to suit narrative ends for which Templeton is condemned, a parallel we might see as self-reflexive but is also a blind spot. In season two's "All Prologue," D'Angelo attends a reading group discussion of *The Great Gatsby* in prison and is told by the leader (novelist Richard Price in cameo) that Fitzgerald said that there "are no second acts in American lives." D'Angelo interprets this through the conventions of naturalism and his own life, suggesting that who you were "first" determines who you can be, that Gatsby's attempt to start anew, like D'Angelo's own brief fantasy of entering witness protection and escaping the drug trade, was never truly possible. This determinism is reflected in the series' finale in which Michael robs one of Marlo's associates, his style of dress and comportment marking him as a reincarnated Omar, while Dukie shoots heroin in an alley, following in Bubble's footsteps, both cycles inevitably continuing. Although less sensationalist than Templeton's embellishments, such narratives risk encouraging us to mourn doomed inner-city lives rather than advocate for social change.

In contrast to Templeton's self-serving style of reporting, aimed at winning him a Pulitzer, is Mike Fletcher (Brandon Young), who is instructed by responsible editor Gus Haynes to find a story worth telling and stick with it for a period of time, without worrying about what he will write until he has a full understanding of the situation, and then to "write it like it feels" ("Took"). Fletcher spends time with Bubbles, now over a year clean from drug addiction, to learn the reality of those who survive homelessness in Baltimore. The story Fletcher eventually writes—of Bubbles's redemption, which we have viewed—is praised by Gus for being a valuable and true piece of journalism that conveys a "real sense of place" and finds "drama in small moments" ("Clarifications"). It is explicitly contrasted with the shallow and sensationalist story written by Templeton based on spending one night sleeping in a homeless encampment. After

Bubbles reads the story when Fletcher seeks his approval to publish, he asks, "What good is a story like that?"; the answer is that "people read it, think about it; maybe see things different" ("-30-"). The stories Fletcher tells are the sort responsible journalists should strive to tell, and I argue they also represent what Simon and Burns have striven to achieve with *The Wire*.

A full assessment of the series, however, requires a more dialectical view. Although *The Wire* provides a detailed, nuanced, and socially complex portrait of the Baltimore drug trade and its economic causes and social costs (arguably with more context and understanding than nonfictional accounts), the series nonetheless cannot be reduced to either replacing bankrupt journalism or providing insights through the "drama in small moments." These stories of lives of drug addicts, of corner boys who aspire to become kings rather than remain pawns, and of inner-city men whose only path to financial security and meaningful work is the drug trade are important to the series, but *The Wire* gains its audience in part because other aspects are more conventional: the police investigations, the wars between rival gangs, the shoot-outs and murders, the cool gangster ambiance and style. *The Wire's* greater popular success than Simon's series *Treme* (HBO 2010–), which similarly provides a complex depiction of lives in New Orleans and the consequences of the government's discriminatory policies, is perhaps explained by the absence in the later series of a recognizable genre formula upon which to hang its narratives.

In these respects, *The Wire* is perhaps dangerously close to the sensationalized journalism disparaged in season five but with two key differences that distinguish it not only from counterfeit journalism but also from previous police dramas. First, although it provides many of the conventional pleasures of such series, it does not provide *only* these but instead combines them with stories that enrich our contextual understanding of crime. Second, although it fictionalizes and shapes its stories, adds flare through characters such as Omar, and combines its

Rust-belt Baltimore—the real protagonist

grim realism with more wit and humor than is likely typical of a day in the life of a Baltimore street corner, *The Wire* nonetheless begins from a deep and personal understanding of the places and the people it narrates: it embellishes with fiction and the techniques of good writing, but it does not *invent* its world. The series cannot be understood simply as a police drama—even an innovative one—but simultaneously cannot be understood as entirely divorced from that format.

Rather, *The Wire* combines journalism and fiction: the positive consequence is careful attention to detail and context characteristic of responsible journalism, enhanced by the emotional power of narratives to compel audience attention and (com)passion; but this strength is simultaneously shadowed by a tendency to allow narrative priorities to dominate, resulting in a vision of Baltimore that viewers may take to be the whole city but from which have been erased signs of hope (such as successful community activism) to achieve the emotional impact of tragedy. *The Wire's* innovative use of the police drama format enables it to tell a more truthful story about crime, revising a genre that has been used to reinforce simplistic law-and-order, tough-on-crime ideology. *The Wire* also pushes the genre of television toward the richness of narrative film in stories told over a time frame that merges film's visual capacity with the scope of long-form narrative fiction. Fredric Jameson sees in this combination a unique achievement that cannot be found in most other mass-cultural narratives, "a plot in which Utopian elements are introduced, without fantasy or wish fulfilment, into the construction of the fictive, yet utterly realistic, events" (371).

The Wire is an important text documenting the reality of neoliberalism and the damage it has caused to American inner cities, predominantly through the drug culture. For this reason alone, it stands as an important text of our times, a milestone for a television series to have achieved this prominent position as celebrated text of social critique. Discussing the power of television as a medium and praising the British social realist tradition, Nelson argues, "a drama that convinces an audience of the existence of formerly untold ills within a society might go further to raise awareness of the inequalities and injustices inherent in the very structure of society and, accordingly, promote fundamental social change" (171). The question of whether *The Wire* has been able to produce meaningful social change is difficult to answer: the hope that it has opened the eyes of its viewers to a reality they previously did not recognize is articulated both within the diegesis and beyond it. This relationship between fiction and the social reality *The Wire* depicts has also been important to the actors who worked on the show. Based on his experiences, for example, Jermaine Crawford, who played Dukie, went on to make a documentary called *Teenager Homelessness in America: A Change Is Gonna Come* (Alvarez 167); Sonja Sohn, who played Kima, founded a charity called Re-

Wired for Change that works with at-risk youth in Baltimore through educational programs and street-based interventions. The emotional investment *The Wire* compels can translate into a desire to work for social change, but it does not necessarily produce this result. Erika Johnson-Lewis suggests that its long-form serial narrative works against optimism because "it wallows far too long in the decay and dejection of contemporary urban life revealing the general conclusion of the entire series: the more things change, the more they stay the same."

I maintain that the more important issue is the audience's complicity in the systems that *The Wire* critiques. Daniel Mc-Neil points out that an embrace of the culture of those dispossessed by mainstream economic forces has not historically translated into valuing the lives of those whose culture is so celebrated. The more important insight, he argues, is that as long as *The Wire's* viewers "seize the homes and poses of the previous

Nick contemplates the end of his way of life as the union is decertified.

owners, buy condos on the docks and ripped stevedore T-shirts at vintage outlets, and cast a nostalgic glance at white fans of hip hop who sincerely believe it's a question of where you're at rather than where you're from," people like those depicted in the series will continue to be "engulfed by American myth and myopia." Thus real social change will become possible only if *The Wire*'s audiences recognize the series as more than the compelling television it clearly is and are willing to accept that the larger context it brings to our understanding of crime includes our own choices, however distant they may seem at first glance.

Introduction

1 Other critics have also noted these novelistic tendencies. See Scandalum Magnatum, Klein, Love, Vest

2 In a lecture delivered at Birkbeck College on February 24, 2012 (available at http://backdoorbroadcasting.net/2012/02/slavoj-zizek-the-wire-or-the-clash-of-civilisations-in-one-country/), Slavoj Žižek argues that the series' conclusion, which shows the struggle against fate to be futile, reinforces rather than challenges capitalism. A preferable response, he argues, is not to suggest ways to worry about the failures of this system but instead to let the system itself fully break, thereby creating a space for something new to emerge

Chapter 1

"It's America, man" is the last line of dialogue in the prologue of the first episode, "The Target." It is the answer a witness gives McNulty to the question of why they did not just refuse to include a man in their poker game given his history of trying to steal the money: in America, you have to let people play

1 John Kraniauskas reads The Wire through this framework but argues that its insistent incorporation of more and more of the social context of crime into its world "threatens to overload and diffuse its televisual *focus* on what is most compelling: the dramatization of the political

economy of crime as the key to the understanding of contemporary neoliberal capitalist society (in Baltimore) and its policing" (26).

2 Sara Taylor makes the important point that HBO is part of the neoliberalism that is critiqued by the show, part of transforming global cultures into market cultures. Thus *The Wire's* very existence is fundamentally dependent upon precisely the structures it critiques. This political economy perspective is underrepresented in most critical responses to the show. Simon acknowledges that freedom from advertisers enabled him to tell stories incompatible with the need to "sell sports utility vehicles and pre-washed jeans to all the best demographics" (Alvarez 12), but he fails to consider that HBO is also a profitable corporation, gaining its capital from sources other than advertising.

3 Klein argues further that in invoking the conventions of melodrama but then refusing to grant the cathartic emotional affect generally associated with this form, *The Wire* produces an active, socially engaged viewer rather than the passive spectator of melodrama. Thus, she argues, *The Wire* uses such conventions in a way more likely to produce changed social action in the world external to the text.

4 See Vest, and Gibb and Sabin for a more detailed analysis

5 "Late Editions," in an exchange between fourteen-year-old protagonists Dukie (Jermaine Crawford) and Michael (Tristan Wilds), includes an allusion to *Dexter* (2006–) that further comments on the gap between most television viewing and the reality of life in Baltimore. Dukie and Michael are living alone, caring for Michael's younger brother, abandoned by their drug-addicted parents. Michael supports them through his work as an enforcer for Marlo; he has become targeted himself, as Marlo suspects Michael has leaked information to the police, and Michael has just killed the person sent to kill him, Snoop As Michael rushes into their home in a panic to move Dukie and his brother before they are found, Dukie is watching television and tries to explain to Michael the appeal of a show in which a serial killer only kills other serial killers. The gap between such fantasies of murder and their circumstances is evident.

6 In their book on the contemporary U.S prison system, *Punishment for Sale,* Donna Selman and Paul Leighton argue that just as the contemporary drug culture of criminality cannot be understood without tracing the money from the street level to the corporate level of those who benefit, it is also necessary to "follow the money" to understand

the changing culture of mandatory sentencing that benefits corporations that have entrenched themselves in core areas of the criminal justice system.

7 See Sean Michael Robinson and Joy DeLyria for a witty counterfactual account of *The Wire* as Victorian serial that includes a prose rendering of this scene in period style that retains the original dialogue.

Chapter 2

1 Further, the county-city divisions of wealth that are central to the political themes of season three are also, to a large extent, racial politics of a white county and black city that were produced by this pattern of settlement. Pietila notes, "escaping the city's racial cauldron could not have been easier, an invisible jurisdictional fence ran just a few miles from City Hall. On the other side was Baltimore County, an independent entity with its own government, laws, rules, traditions—and a tax rate half of the city. So many whites fled there between 1950 and 1970 that the county's population more than doubled, from 270,273 to 621,077" (loc 2265–67).

2 Similarly, the large Jewish community of Baltimore and the role of Jewish residents as "intermediary" between white and black cultures are not present in the series. A single series cannot, of course, represent all facets of life in the city and there are other absences as well, but this failure to engage fully with historical anti-Semitism (indeed, a prejudice reinforced by the show's characterization of unethical defense attorney Levy as Jewish) is an important and damaging oversight. The issue of how the few Jewish characters on the show are represented is discussed by Kahn-Harris

3 Macek draws on quantitative research published by Jimmie Reeves and Richard Campbell, published in *Cracked Coverage: Television News, the Anti-Cocaine Crusade, and the Reagan Legacy* (1994). Selman and Leighton also credit this period of news reporting and popular culture images with the massive rise in incarceration in the United States, making it the country with not only the highest per capita incarceration rate in the world but also the most racially targeted sentencing laws.

4 "We might have saved ourselves from the psychic cost of the drug war—the utter alienation of an underclass from its government, the wedding of that alienation to a ruthless economic engine, and finally, the birth of an outlaw philosophy as ugly and enraged as hate and despair can produce—if we had embraced the common sense that

comes with the paper bag" (Simon and Burns 160).

5 Avon says to Stringer, "You were all heavy into that black pride bullshit" ("Straight and True"), but it is never made clear either why Avon regards this as bullshit or why the aspiration to own grocery stores was more consistent with a vision of black pride than the militancy of Avon's youth. The failure to engage with the community politics of black activism as an alternative to entering the drug trade is one of the ways that the series is compromised by a privileging of narrative requirements and thus somewhat limited in its ability to offer a full, realist representation of Baltimore

6 Peter Clandfield argues, "precisely because he seems to be without Stringer's desire for legitimacy, his prospective involvement with real estate underlines the critique of urban redevelopment in *The Wire* as an industry driven by amoral pursuit of profit rather than by principle" (48)

Chapter 3

1 The original source is Simon's narrative *Homicide* and actual practice in the Baltimore police department.

2 James Peterson argues, "Bodie challenges the Horatio Alger narrative of drug dealing and hustling. His hard work, loyalty, and heart do not allow him to achieve the economic spoils of his bosses" (112).

3 A similar pattern is evident in the casting of two of Mayor Carcetti's advisors, the African American Norman (Reg E. Cathey), his campaign manager who deeply resents Carcetti's decision not to take state money for schools, and his white chief of staff Michael (Neal Huff), who advises him to do so. Race is not explicitly discussed as a motivation for differing attitudes in either case, but the casting is suggestive

4 Melvin Williams, the drug dealer upon whom the character of Avon was based, supports this reading of a changed culture of drug distribution between the 1980s and the present. during his era, he claims, murder "meant something"; "Now it's just your shoes are wrong, bang, you're dead" (qtd in Alvarez 109). Kenneth Durr directly connects the greater degree of violent crime associated with the drug trade to the loss of work through deindustrialization elsewhere in the city, although he notes that the increase in crime was out of proportion with the pace of deindustrialization: "In the 1950s shoplifting had been the preferred means of supporting a habit, but by the late 1960s it had given way to burglary and violent crime. In Baltimore

City from 1965 to 1970, burglaries tripled and robberies quintupled" (loc. 2927–31)

Chapter 4

1 Vest credits George Pelecanos with this insight and with writing the story line about Tosha's death (200).

2 Its contemporary series *The Shield* does much better in this regard, including as central characters an experienced and principled detective, Claudette Wymns (CCH Pounder), and a uniformed officer, Dani Sofer (Catherine Dent). Both characters are complexly realized, and the challenges presented by their gender in this environment are neither ignored nor made the focus of their screen time The heart of this show, too, however, remains the male characters. *The Closer* (2005–) features a strong female lead, but almost all of its supporting cast are male

WORKS CITED

Alvarez, Rafael *The Wire Truth Be Told.* New York: Canongate, 2009.

Anderson, Angela "No Such Thing as Good and Evil: *The Wire* and the Humanization of the Object of Risk in the Age of Biopolitics." *Dark Matter* 4 (May 29, 2009). http://www.darkmatter101 org/site/2009/05/29/no-such-thing-as-good-and-evil-the-wire-and-the-humanization-of-the-object-of-risk-in-the-age-of-biopolitics/ (accessed March 15, 2011).

Atlas, John, and Peter Dreier. "Is *The Wire* Too Cynical?" *Dissent* (Summer 2008): 79–82.

Beck, Richard. "Beyond the Choir· An Interview with David Simon " *Film Quarterly* 62 2 (2008): 44–49.

Beliveau, Ralph, and Laura Bolf-Beliveau. "Posing Problems and Picking Fights: Critical Pedagogy and the Corner Boys." In *The Wire: Urban Decay and American Television,* ed. T. Potter and C W Marshall, 91–105 New York: Continuum, 2009

Benn Michaels, Walter. "Going Boom." *bookforum.com* (February/March 2009). http://www.bookforum.com/inprint/015_05/3274 (accessed March 24, 2011).

Bonnycastle, Kevin Denys. "Not the Usual Suspects: The Obfuscation of Political Economy and Race in *CSI*." *The CSI Effect: Television, Crime, and Governance,* ed. Michele Myers and Val Marie Johnson, 149–76. Lanham, MD: Lexington, 2009.

Burkeman, Oliver "Arrogant? Moi?" *The Guardian,* March 28, 2009. http://www.guardian.co.uk/media/2009/mar/28/david-simon-the-wire-interview (accessed March 21, 2011)

Burns, Ed, Dennis Lehane, George Pelecanos, Richard Price, and David Simon. "*The Wire's* War on the Drug War." *Time,* March 5, 2008 http://www.time.com/time/nation/article/0,8599,1719872,00.html (accessed March 3, 2011)

Byers, Michele, and Val Marie Johnson. "*CSI* as Neoliberalism: An Introduction." In *The CSI Effect: Television, Crime and Governance,* xiii–xxxvi New York: Lexington, 2009

Chaddha, Anmol, William Julius Wilson, and Sudhir A. Venkatesh. "In Defense of *The Wire.*" *Dissent* (Summer 2008): 83–86.

Clandfield, Peter. "'We Ain't Got No Yard': Crime, Development and Urban Environment." In *The Wire: Urban Decay and American Television,* ed. T Potter and C W Marshall, 37–49. New York: Continuum, 2009

Cook, Brian. "Joys of *The Wire* " *In These Times,* February 22, 2008. http://www.inthesetimes.com/article/3525/joys_of_the_wire/ (accessed March 25, 2011).

Covington, Jeanette. *Crime and Racial Constructions. Cultural Misinformation about African Americans in Media and Academia.* Lanham, MD: Lexington, 2010

Creeber, Glen *Serial Television: Big Drama on the Small Screen.* London: BFI, 2004.

Davis, Mike. *City of Quartz Excavating the Future in Los Angeles.* London: Verso, 2006

Dobson, Nicholas "Generic Difference and Innovation in *CSI. Crime Scene Investigation.*" In *The CSI Effect: Television, Crime, and Governance,* ed. Michele Myers and Val Marie Johnson, 75–89. Lanham, MD: Lexington, 2009.

Dunn, Anne. "The Genres of Television." In *Narrative and Media* by Helen Fulton with Rosemary Huisman, Julian Murphet, and Anne Dunn, 125–39 Cambridge. Cambridge University Press, 2005.

Durr, Kenneth D. *Behind the Backlash: White Working-Class Politics in Baltimore, 1940–1980.* Kindle ed. Chapel Hill: University of North Carolina Press, 2007.

Ellis, John. "Television as Working-Through." In *Television and Common Knowledge,* ed. Jostein Gripsrud, 55–70. London Routledge, 1999

Fugle, Sophie. "Short Circuiting the Power Grid: *The Wire* as Critique of Institutional Power." *Dark Matter* 4 (May 29, 2009) http://www.darkmatter101.org/site/2009/05/29/short-circuiting-the-power-grid-the-wire-as-critique-of-institutional-power/ (accessed March 15, 2011)

Gibb, Jane, and Roger Sabin. "Who Loves Ya, David Simon?" *Dark Matter* 4 (May 29, 2009) http.//www.darkmatter101.org/site/2009/05/29/who-loves-ya-david-simon/ (accessed March 15, 2011)

Hall, Stuart, Chas Critcher, Tony Jefferson, John N. Clarke, and Brian Roberts. *Policing the Crisis Mugging, the State and Law and Order* London Palgrave, 1978.

Harvey, David. *Social Justice and the City* Rev ed. Athens· University of Georgia Press, 2009.

Hsu, Hua. "Walking in Someone Else's City: *The Wire* and the Limits of Empathy." *Criticism* 52.3/5 (2010): 509–28

Jameson, Fredric. "Realism and Utopia in *The Wire*." *Criticism* 52.3/5 (2010)· 359–72.

Johnson-Lewis, Erika. "The More Things Change, the More They Stay the Same: Serial Narrative on *The Wire*." *Dark Matter* 4 (May 29, 2009). http://www.darkmatter101 org/site/2009/05/29/the-more-things-change-the-more-they-stay-the-same-serial-narrative-on-the-wire/ (accessed March 15, 2011)

Kahn-Harris, Keith. "The Politics of Brisket: Jews and *The Wire* " *Dark Matter* 4 (May 29, 2009) http://www darkmatter101.org/site/2009/05/29/the-politics-of-brisket-jews-and-the-wire/ (accessed March 15, 2011)

Kelly, Lisa W. "Casting *The Wire*: Complicating Notions of Performance, Authenticity, and 'Otherness.'" *Dark Matter* 4 (May 29, 2009) http // www darkmatter101.org/site/wp-content/uploads/pdf/4_Kelly_%20 Casting_The_Wire.pdf (accessed March 15, 2011).

Klein, Amanda Ann. "'The Dickensian Aspect': Melodrama, Viewer Engagement, and the Socially Conscious Text." In *The Wire: Urban Decay and American Television,* ed. T. Potter and C. W. Marshall, 177–89. New York. Continuum, 2009.

Kraniauskas, John. "Elasticity of Demand Reflection on *The Wire*." *Radical Philosophy* 154 (March/April 2009)· 25–34.

La Berge, Leigh Claire. "Capitalist Realism and the Serial Form The Fifth Season of *The Wire*." *Criticism* 52.3/5 (2010): 547–67.

LeBesco, Kathleen. "'Gots to Get Got'· Social Justice and Audience Response to Omar Little." In *The Wire: Urban Decay and American Television,* ed T. Potter and C W. Marshall, 217–31. New York. Continuum, 2009.

Love, Chris. "Greek Gods in Baltimore· Greek Tragedy and *The Wire* " *Criticism* 52.3/5 (2010). 487–507.

Macek, Steve *Urban Nightmares: The Media, the Right, and the Moral Panic over the City.* Minneapolis. University of Minnesota Press, 2006.

Marshall, Courtenay D. "Barksdale Women Crime, Empire and the Production of Gender." In *The Wire. Urban Decay and American Television,* ed. T. Potter and C. W. Marshall, 149–61. New York: Continuum, 2009

McMillan, Alasdair. "Heroism, Institutions and the Police Procedural." In *The Wire· Urban Decay and American Television,* ed. T. Potter and C. W. Marshall, 50–63 New York. Continuum, 2009.

McNeil, Daniel "White Negroes and *The Wire.*" *Dark Matter* 4 (May 29, 2009). http.//www.darkmatter101.org/site/2009/05/29/white-negroes-and-the-wire/ (accessed March 15, 2011).

Mittell, Jason. *Genre and Television: From Cop Shows to Cartoons in American Culture.* New York: Routledge, 2004.

Morley, David. "Finding Out about the World from Television News: Some Difficulties." In *Television and Common Knowledge,* ed. Jostein Gripsrud, 135–57 London: Routledge, 1999.

Nelson, Robin. *State of Play· Contemporary "High-End" TV drama* Manchester: Manchester University Press, 2007

Pearson, Felicia *Grace after Midnight: A Memoir.* New York: Grand Central, 2007.

Peterson, James Braxton. "Corner-Boy Masculinity: Intersections of Inner-City Manhood." In *The Wire: Urban Decay and American Television,* ed T. Potter and C. W. Marshall, 107–21. New York: Continuum, 2009

Pietila, Antero. *Not in My Neighborhood: How Bigotry Shaped a Great American City.* Kindle ed. Lanham, MD: Ivan R. Dee, 2010

Potter, Tiffany, and C W Marshall. "'I Am the American Dream': Modern Urban Tragedy and the Borders of Fiction." In *The Wire: Urban Decay and American Television,* ed. T. Potter and C. W. Marshall, 1–14. New York: Continuum, 2009.

———, eds. *The Wire: Urban Decay and American Television.* New York: Continuum, 2009.

Robinson, Sean Michael, and Joy DeLyria. "'When It's Not Your Turn'. The Quintessentially Victorian Vision of Ogden's 'The Wire.'" *The Hooded Utilitarian* March 23, 2011. http://hoodedutilitarian.com/2011/03/when-its-not-your-turn-the-quintessentially-victorian-vision-of-ogdens-the-wire/ (accessed March 28, 2011).

Ryan, Andrew. "It Made Sense to Finish the Show with a Reflection on the State of Media." *The Globe and Mail,* January 4, 2008, R3

(Scandalum Magnatum) Mike (blogger). "Balzac of Baltimore." *Scan-*

dalum Magnatum, January 13, 2008, http //scandalum.wordpress. com/2008/01/13/balzac-of-baltimore/ (accessed March 5, 2011)

Selman, Donna, and Paul Leighton *Punishment for Sale: Private Prisons, Big Business, and the Incarceration Binge* Kindle ed. Lanham, MD. Rowman and Littlefield, 2010

Sheehan, Helena, and Sheamus Sweeney. "*The Wire* and the World: Narrative and Metanarrative." *Jump Cut* (51). http://www.ejumpcut org/ archive/jc51.2009/Wire/index html (accessed March 5, 2011).

Siano, Maria. *The People Are Represented. A Discourse Analysis of Contemporary Programs in the Television Crime Genre.* Youngstown, NY: Teneo, 2008.

Simon, David. "Death of the Newspaperman." *In These Times,* July 2009, 15–17

———. "A Final Thank You to 'Wire' Fans " *HBO* March 10, 2008. http:// www hbo.com/thewire/finaletter (accessed February 1, 2009).

———. *Homicide: A Year on the Killing Streets* Boston· Houghton Mifflin, 1991.

———. Introduction to *The Wire: Truth Be Told,* by Rafael Alvarez, 1–31. New York: Canongate, 2009.

Simon, David, and Ed Burns. *The Corner: A Year in the Life of an Inner-City Neighborhood* New York Broadway, 1997.

Speidel, Linda. "'Thin Line 'tween heaven and here' (Bubbles): Real and Imagined Space in *The Wire*." *Dark Matter* 4 (May 29, 2009). http //www. darkmatter101.org/site/2009/05/29/thin-line-tween-heaven-and-here-bubbles-real-and-imagined-space-in-the-wire/ (accessed March 15, 2011).

Taylor, Sara. "*The Wire*· Investigating the Use of a Neoliberal Institutional Apparatus and a 'New Humanist' Philosophical Apparatus." *Dark Matter* 4 (May 29, 2009). http://www.darkmatter101 org/ site/2009/05/29/the-wire-investigating-the-use-of-a-neoliberal-institutional-apparatus-and-a-new-humanist-philosophical-apparatus/ (accessed March 15, 2011)

Toscano, Alberta, and Jeff Kinkle. "Baltimore as World and Representation Cognitive Mapping and Capitalism in *The Wire*." *Dossier,* April 8, 2009 http //dossierjournal com/read/theory/baltimore-as-world-and-representation-cognitive-mapping-and-capitalism-in-the-wire/ (accessed March 12, 2011)

Venkatesh, Sudhir *American Project: The Rise and Fall of a Modern Ghetto* Kindle ed. Cambridge, MA: Harvard University Press, 2002.

————. *Off the Books: The Underground Economy of the Urban Poor.* Cambridge, MA: Harvard University Press, 2006

Vest, Jason. *The Wire, Deadwood, Homicide, and NYPD Blue: Violence Is Power.* Santa Barbara: Praeger, 2011.

Weisberg, Jacob "*The Wire* on Fire: Analyzing the Best Show on Television." *Slate* September 13, 2006 http://www.slate.com/id/2149566/ (accessed March 5, 2011).

Wilson, David. *Cities and Race America's New Black Ghetto* Kindle ed New York: Routledge, 2006.

www.ingramcontent.com/pod-product-compliance
Lightning Source LLC
Chambersburg PA
CBHW052137270326
41930CB00012B/2921